Child Maltreatment

A Developmental Psychopathology Approach

Kathryn Becker-Blease and Patricia K. Kerig

AMERICAN PSYCHOLOGICAL ASSOCIATION
WASHINGTON, DC

Copyright © 2016 by the American Psychological Association. All rights reserved. Except as permitted under the United States Copyright Act of 1976, no part of this publication may be reproduced or distributed in any form or by any means, including, but not limited to, the process of scanning and digitization, or stored in a database or retrieval system, without the prior written permission of the publisher.

Published by
American Psychological Association
750 First Street, NE
Washington, DC 20002
www.apa.org

To order
APA Order Department
P.O. Box 92984
Washington, DC 20090-2984
Tel: (800) 374-2721; Direct: (202) 336-5510
Fax: (202) 336-5502; TDD/TTY: (202) 336-6123
Online: www.apa.org/pubs/books
E-mail: order@apa.org

In the U.K., Europe, Africa, and the Middle East, copies may be ordered from
American Psychological Association
3 Henrietta Street
Covent Garden, London
WC2E 8LU England

Typeset in Minion by Circle Graphics, Inc., Columbia, MD

Printer: Maple Press, York, PA
Cover Designer: Berg Design, Albany, NY

The opinions and statements published are the responsibility of the authors, and such opinions and statements do not necessarily represent the policies of the American Psychological Association.

Library of Congress Cataloging-in-Publication Data

Names: Becker-Blease, Kathryn, author. | Kerig, Patricia, author.
Title: Child maltreatment : a developmental psychopathology approach / Kathryn Becker-Blease and Patricia K. Kerig.
Description: First edition. | Washington, DC : American Psychological Association, [2016] | Series: Concise guides on trauma care book series | Includes bibliographical references and index.
Identifiers: LCCN 2015042238 | ISBN 9781433822216 | ISBN 1433822210
Subjects: LCSH: Child abuse—Psychological aspects. | Abused children—Mental health. | Psychic trauma in children—Treatment.
Classification: LCC RC569.5.C55 B335 2016 | DDC 616.85/8223—dc23 LC record available at http://lccn.loc.gov/2015042238

British Library Cataloguing-in-Publication Data
A CIP record is available from the British Library.

Printed in the United States of America
First Edition

http://dx.doi.org/10.1037/14898-000

Child Maltreatment

Concise Guides
on Trauma Care Book Series

Treating PTSD With Cognitive-Behavioral Therapies: Interventions That Work
  Candice M. Monson and Philippe Shnaider

Child Maltreatment: A Developmental Psychopathology Approach
  Kathryn Becker-Blease and Patricia K. Kerig

Contents

Series Foreword	*vii*
Anne DePrince and Ann T. Chu	
1. Maltreatment From a Developmental Psychopathology Perspective	3
2. Infant and Toddler Maltreatment	19
3. Maltreatment of Preschool-Age Children	37
4. Maltreatment in Middle Childhood	55
5. Maltreatment in Adolescence	73
6. Emerging Adulthood	91
Afterword	103
Appendix	105
References	117
Index	147
About the Authors	161

Series Foreword

Exposure to traumatic events is all too common, increasing the risk for a range of significant mental problems, such as posttraumatic stress disorder (PTSD) and depression; physical health problems; negative health behaviors, such as smoking and excessive alcohol consumption; impaired social and occupational functioning; and overall lower quality of life. As mass traumas (e.g., September 11, military engagements in Iraq and Afghanistan, natural disasters such as Hurricane Katrina) have propelled trauma into a brighter public spotlight, the number of trauma survivors seeking services for mental health consequences will likely increase. Yet despite the far-ranging consequences of trauma and the high rates of exposure, relatively little emphasis is placed on trauma education in undergraduate and graduate training programs for mental health service providers in the United States. Calls for action have appeared in the American Psychological Association's journal *Psychological Trauma: Theory, Research, Practice, and Policy* with such articles as "The Need for Inclusion of Psychological Trauma in the Professional Curriculum: A Call to Action" by Christine A. Courtois and Steven N. Gold (2009) and "The Art and Science of Trauma-Focused Training and Education" by Anne P. DePrince and Elana Newman (2011). The lack of education in the assessment and treatment of trauma-related distress and associated clinical issues at undergraduate and graduate levels increases the urgency to develop effective trauma resources for students as well as postgraduate professionals.

SERIES FOREWORD

This book series, Concise Guides on Trauma Care, addresses that urgent need by providing truly translational books that bring the best of trauma psychology science to mental health professionals working in diverse settings. To do so, the series focuses on what we know (and do not know) about specific trauma topics, with attention to how trauma psychology science translates to diverse populations (diversity broadly defined, in terms of development, ethnicity, socioeconomic status, sexual orientation, and so forth).

This series represents one of many efforts by Division 56 (Trauma Psychology) of the American Psychological Association to advance trauma training and education (e.g., see http://www.apatraumadivision.org/78/resources.html). We are pleased to work with Division 56 and a volunteer editorial board to develop this series, which continues with the publication of this important book on child maltreatment from a developmental psychopathology perspective by Kathryn Becker-Blease and Patricia K. Kerig. Becker-Blease and Kerig's book offers an inclusive, practical, and accessible overview of the broad research literature on developmental psychopathology as applicable to children and youth who have been maltreated. Bringing the best of developmental, clinical, and trauma psychological science perspectives to this book, Becker-Blease and Kerig integrate essential information that will be of great use to mental health professionals serving clients who have been maltreated. Future books in the series will build on this foundation to address a range of assessment, treatment, and developmental issues in trauma-informed care.

Anne DePrince
Ann T. Chu
Series Editors

Child Maltreatment

1

Maltreatment From a Developmental Psychopathology Perspective

Child maltreatment is at once a medical, public health, developmental, mental health, and criminal problem. Because of the diligent work of researchers, clinicians, and other professionals from all of these fields over recent decades, we as a society are better equipped to prevent child abuse and intervene to help abused and neglected children. Today, more than ever, children are protected by child protective services, have access to multidisciplinary evaluations through child advocacy centers, and are helped with evidence-based trauma-focused mental health care and even trauma-sensitive schools (J. A. Cohen, Mannarino, & Deblinger, 2012; S. F. Cole, Eisner, Gregory, & Ristuccia, 2013; Cross et al., 2008).

Still, fundamental questions remain. Amid some success, the rate of child abuse and neglect remains stubbornly high overall (Finkelhor, Turner, Ormrod, & Hamby, 2010). The various definitions of child maltreatment used by clinicians, researchers, and the civil and criminal

http://dx.doi.org/10.1037/14898-001
Child Maltreatment: A Developmental Psychopathology Approach, by K. Becker-Blease and P. K. Kerig
Copyright © 2016 by the American Psychological Association. All rights reserved.

legal systems impede progress toward better prevention and intervention (Becker-Blease & Freyd, 2005; Finkelhor, Ormrod, & Turner, 2007). We lack a robust, coherent model of the developmental effects of maltreatment. As an example, the following two quotes, both by scientists, sum up what is known about trauma and resilience for a general audience:

> Even if an abused person comes to terms with the traumatic memories and chooses (for the sake of sanity) to forgive the perpetrator, this will not reverse the neurobiological abnormalities. (Teicher, 2000, p. 66)
>
> A recent study showing how major life traumas affect people suggests that, if it happened over three months ago, with only a few exceptions, it has no impact whatsoever on your happiness. . . . We are wired to be resilient. We're wired to find what's good in the current situation. (D. Gilbert, 2007)

How can two prominent scientists come to seemingly opposite conclusions? The devil really is in the details. These conclusions are not necessarily inconsistent. An abused person conceivably might have a brain that is permanently damaged by maltreatment and yet is plastic enough to change in adaptive ways. Further, an abused person might report the same level of happiness after a major trauma as he or she did before it. Finding out whether either of these suppositions is true, for whom, and how is among the work cut out for developmental psychopathologists.

DEVELOPMENTAL PSYCHOPATHOLOGY TACKLES COMPLEX QUESTIONS ABOUT MALTREATMENT

In this book, our goal is to explain, summarize, and translate the science of developmental psychopathology and the closely related fields of developmental traumatology (De Bellis, 2001) and developmental victimology (Finkelhor & Kendall-Tackett, 1997) for clinicians and other professionals who work with maltreated children and those at risk for maltreatment.

A DEVELOPMENTAL PSYCHOPATHOLOGY PERSPECTIVE

In this chapter, we begin by summarizing the basics of a developmental psychopathology approach. Such an approach requires attention to

1. developmental context—how human development affects the dynamics of child maltreatment;
2. ecological context—the family, community, and society in which child maltreatment occurs;
3. process—the mechanisms through which maltreatment affects people;
4. developmental trajectories—both adaptation and maladaptation over time, in both continuous and discontinuous ways. The same factor may lead to one outcome for one child and a different outcome for another (multifinality), and the same outcome may arise from different factors in different children (equifinality); and
5. how biological, genetic, and environmental factors, including prior development, combine to influence development.

Developmental Context

Developmental psychopathology can be defined as "normal development gone awry" (Kerig, Ludlow, & Wenar, 2012, p. 1). Only by understanding normative development can we understand problems that arise in development. Neglect, for example, is the absence of expected care necessary for children, taking the child's culture, maturity, and environmental risks into account. Normatively, in most of the United States today, children are supervised at least through age 10 and are gradually taught the skills necessary to care for themselves first for short periods and then longer periods until they are capable of independence in late adolescence. However, in the real world, adequately supervising children requires a more nuanced understanding of risk and development. At what age is it safe for the adult responsible to leave a sleeping child alone to run across the street to help a neighbor for a few minutes? To leave a preschooler in the bath to answer the phone? To leave a child who has developmental delay alone? Developmental psychopathologists argue that there is no way to define neglect, or maltreatment in general, without first understanding normative development.

Ecological Context

A developmental psychopathology perspective requires a focus on context. Child maltreatment affects people on so many levels: as societies, communities, families, and individuals. On a societal level, maltreatment is tremendously expensive. One estimate puts the lifetime cost, including health care, child welfare, criminal justice, special education, and loss of productivity costs, per substantiated maltreatment case at $210,012 per nonfatal case, and $1,272,900 per fatal case. That translates to a cost to society of $124 billion for a year's worth of 579,000 new substantiated child abuse cases (Fang, Brown, Florence, & Mercy, 2012). These costs are on par with some of the most expensive physical health conditions, such as stroke and Type 2 diabetes (Centers for Disease Control and Prevention, 2012; see Figure 1.1). This estimate takes into account only those cases that came to the attention of child protection workers, were found to be meet the legal definition of child maltreatment, and in which the child did not die. If we were to take into account the cost of all maltreatment—substantiated and hidden—the cost would go much higher.

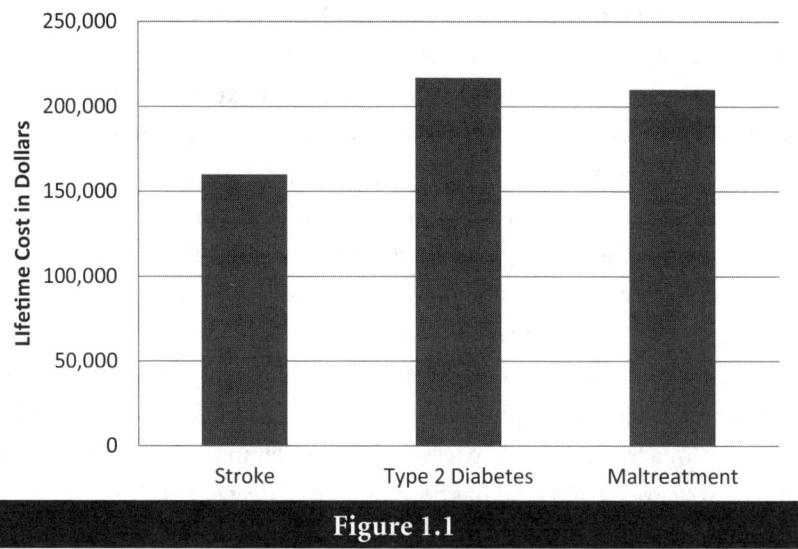

Figure 1.1

The lifetime cost of maltreatment is as costly as other major public health problems. Data from Centers for Disease Control and Prevention (2012).

Society and Communities

The effects of individual cases of maltreatment ripple out in society in ways that are largely hidden. Take, for example, the community's responsibility to protect children from sexual abuse. Schools, churches, camps, day-care facilities, and other youth-serving organizations today—thanks to a combination of best practices, institutional policies, insurance mandates, and laws—recognize the risk of sexual abuse and the requirement to protect children (Gregg & Hansen-Stamp, 2012; Saul & Audage, 2007). Among churches, a cottage industry offers child abuse prevention and response services and training (see, e.g., http://www.reducingtherisk.com and http://www.safechurch.com). For camps, the American Camp Association (ACA) advises:

> Teach your staff to be ever vigilant and question what they see. If just one person had approached Jerry Sandusky[1] when they saw something they thought was inappropriate, his serial child molesting could quite possibly have been stopped much sooner. (ACA Camp Crisis Hotline, 2012)

This vigilance is necessary. Children depend on adults to keep them safe. At the same time, this vigilance takes a toll. It takes time and money to train staff to do this work. It also demands cognitive and emotional resources. It requires not only watching and observing, but also the ability to interpret ambiguous situations and make difficult decisions. In a safer environment, resources can be reallocated, leading to better experiences for children.

Prevention efforts extend to children, and they, too, are affected by the need to be vigilant against potential sex offenders. For example, media coverage of child kidnappings may make children, especially school-age girls, worry about being victims themselves (Becker-Blease, Finkelhor, & Turner, 2008). The same is true of some sexual abuse prevention programs

---

[1] Sandusky is the Pennsylvania State University assistant football coach who was convicted of 45 counts of sexual abuse of boys.

in schools (Finkelhor & Dziuba-Leatherman, 1995; National Sexual Violence Resource Center, 2011). Although some of this worry may be irrational, the fact remains that, given the prevalence of child sexual abuse and imperfect prevention strategies, it is reasonable to be at least somewhat concerned (Finkelhor & Dziuba-Leatherman, 1995). We cannot simply deny the risk. Ultimately, we must reduce the prevalence of abuse in society so that children and those who care for them are able to live freer lives.

Prevention efforts are just one area in which the community as a whole is affected by maltreatment. Maltreatment affects children's development across physical, social/emotional, and cognitive domains. As a result, any organization that works with youth, from day care to college age, will encounter individuals who show signs of child maltreatment that affect their ability to participate and learn, meet behavioral expectations, and relate with other children and staff (S. F. Cole, Greenwald O'Brien, Gadd, Ristuccia, Wallace, & Gregory, 2005; Duncan, 2000).

Family

Families, generally, are organized to protect and nurture their vulnerable members. For this reason, families take on most of the burden of protecting children from maltreatment and caring for children who have been maltreated. The exact functions a family member takes on vary, and it is interesting to consider the breadth of these tasks. Virtually all families take steps to care for their children, although their efforts may be limited, ineffective, or misguided. For example, all but the most neglectful parents spend some effort to ensure their children are not kidnapped, neglected, or abused by other adults. In some families, these activities extend much further to researching the practices of potential children's programs, creating child ID kits for police in the case of abduction, and monitoring children's Internet and cell phone communications, for example. In many communities, these activities seem as common as putting on sunscreen and seatbelts, but the need for this work would plummet if we were able to reduce the threat of maltreatment in the first place.

When children are abused, families are often profoundly affected. When a child is abused by non–family members, the abuse affects the entire family. Family members must come to terms with their own feelings of anger, guilt, and sadness and decide whether and how to navigate the civil and criminal justice systems, as well as how to heal. In other cases, the perpetrator is a family member. When children disclose abuse at the hands of a parent, nonoffending parents report having to move homes, loss of income, loss of support from friends and family, and employment problems (Massat & Lundy, 1998). Sometimes, no parents are able to care for children, and extended family step in to become primary caregivers. More than 2.5 million grandparents are caring for children whose parents are unable to care for them (AARP, n.d.). This experience varies widely, with grandparents reporting exposure to drug-related crime, financial and legal problems, stress and mental health problems, and difficulty finding time to take care of their own health, as well as some benefits stemming from their closer relationships with their grandchildren and living a more active lifestyle (Bailey, Haynes, & Letiecq, 2013; Grinstead, Leder, Jensen, & Bond, 2003; Hayslip & Smith, 2013).

Later in life, young people face the challenge of finding partners and creating new families. A history of maltreatment affects interpersonal relationships as this process unfolds. A history of child maltreatment is associated with later perpetration and victimization in adolescent bullying, gender-based harassment, and dating violence (Wolfe, Crooks, Chiodo, & Jaffe, 2009). The high prevalence of child abuse means that many young adults date, marry, and eventually parent with a partner who experienced maltreatment. These relationships are often difficult (Davis & Petretic-Jackson, 2000).

Developmental and Psychological Processes

Understanding the complexity and systemic nature of child maltreatment is useful for considering the process through which maltreatment affects individuals. Too often, the media focus on individual stories of triumph or tragedy, but the process through which the resilience grows into triumph or unfortunate events compound into tragedy over time is left underexplored. Here is one extended case example that many readers will recognize. Dave Pelzer is the internationally best-selling author of a series of books about his abusive childhood and lifelong recovery. The books are sometimes billed as the story of how a person with unusual traits individually overcame horrific abuse. In keeping with the popular theme of emphasizing an immutable quality of successful individuals, the back cover of one highlights Dave Pelzer's "ultimate act of self-reliance" (Pelzer, 2010). Further, the official Dave Pelzer website headline reads "a living testament of a self-made man" (http://www.davepelzer.com). It is a story of independence, without doubt, in part. But it is also a story of interdependence. The back cover features a quotation from a review of the book by John Bradshaw, who notes the "unique love and dedication that social services and foster families provide for our children in peril." Pelzer (2010) dedicated the book to his wife, "the lady who gave her all to make me the man I am today," and his son, who has "changed my life for the better." The individual narrative only goes so far. In addition, we must consider the social, interpersonal, and developmental processes, unfolding over time and in a variety of contexts that gave rise to the resilient person we see today. On talk shows, made-for-TV movies, and popular books, but also in professional books and journal articles, we wonder: What is different about those who do and do not possess the capacity for success, between those who are resilient or are not resilient? This is a fine question, and one developmental psychopathologists expand to include another: What is it about families, communities, and societies that allow for such incredible personal growth in some individuals who have experienced maltreatment?

We do not yet have the full answer, but we do know that resilience is not just a capacity that someone possesses (or does not possess). Resilience is a complex *process* that evolves over time in different contexts. Recovery is not so much crossing a finish line into a life without symptoms. It is more lifelong growth in the capacity of survivors to meet their own needs and the needs of those who depend on them. Child maltreatment survivors and those who work with them have recognized this complexity. In fact, Dave Pelzer's newest book directly addresses this complexity in defining resilience over the lifespan. The publisher summarizes his latest book, *Too Close to Me: The Middle-Aged Consequences of Revealing a Child Called "It"* (Pelzer, 2014) this way:

> As a child, Pelzer was beaten, starved, and abused both emotionally and physically by his alcoholic and mentally unstable mother. As a man, Pelzer went on to have love, happiness, a fulfilling career, and his own family. To many, Pelzer seemed to have found his happy ending. But for a child abuse survivor, living a normal adult life carries challenges and complications above and beyond those faced by most people. This book, the fifth in Pelzer's nonfiction series, provides an honest and courageous look at the difficulties inherent in marriage, parenthood, work, and life from the perspective of someone who survived horrific physical and emotional terrors as a child—and who seeks to meet the responsibilities and complications of adult life with love, strength, and an open heart.

In it, readers learn that despite success by many measures, life as a middle-aged abuse survivor is still marked by difficulty trusting others, fear, shame, and guilt. Achieving a relative lack of symptoms or relative professional or individual success does not mean that "recovered" abuse survivors are left unchanged. The story is more complex.

Developmental psychopathology offers some useful concepts for helping scientists and practitioners make sense of the complexity inherent in all cases of child maltreatment.

Developmental Trajectories

Maltreatment is associated with an increased risk of mental health problems, violence and criminality, drug addiction, and among other problems, but there is a high degree of variability in outcomes (Finkelhor & Kendall-Tackett, 1997). Child maltreatment survivors, their families, and professionals who work with them often ask themselves to what extent maltreatment led to a given problem and why one person experiences a problem that other child maltreatment survivors do not.

An emphasis on the process through which risk and protective factors work leads to the study of *developmental trajectories. Multifinality*

(Figure 1.2a) refers to the fact that maltreatment can lead to many different outcomes; *equifinality* (Figure 1.2b) refers to the fact that many pathways can lead to a common maltreatment outcome.

Understanding the process through which sexual abuse leads to sexual offending is crucial for effectively understanding, preventing, and intervening in the area of sexual abuse. It is certain that some basic problem

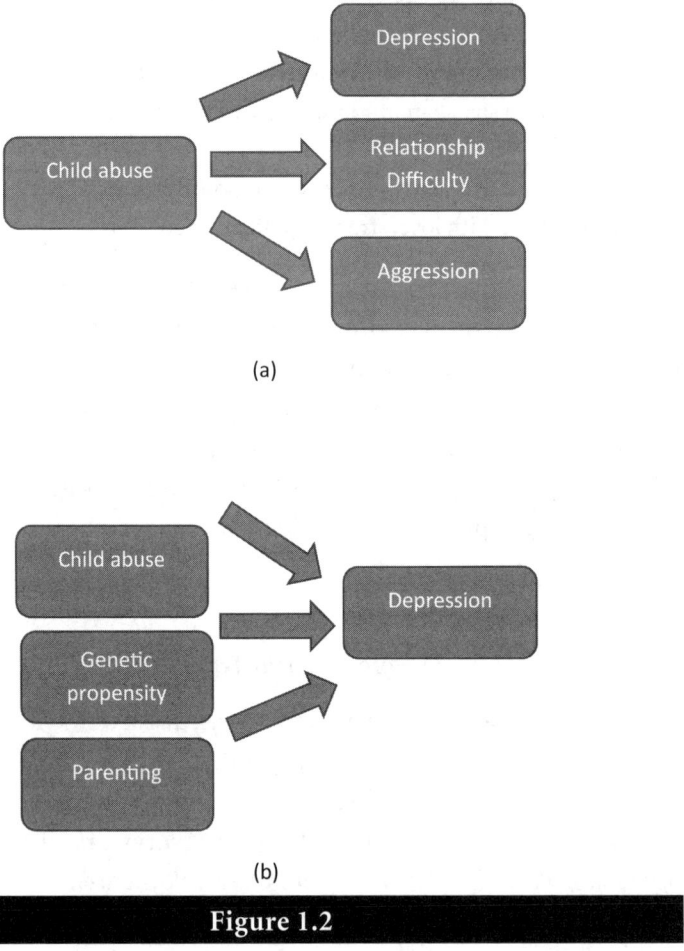

Figure 1.2

(a) Child abuse leads to many different outcomes, an example of *multifinality*. (b) Many different factors, including child abuse, lead to an outcome of depression, an example of *equifinality*.

A DEVELOPMENTAL PSYCHOPATHOLOGY PERSPECTIVE

in sexual functioning is involved in much sexual abuse. Around adolescence, rather than becoming aroused by mutually satisfying sexual activity with peers, some people associate sexual arousal with prepubescent bodies or control and violence. Once this association is made, it can be difficult to extinguish, and treatment is difficult (L. J. Cohen & Galynker, 2002). However, a basic sexual arousal to prepubescent bodies is not the only problem that can result in sexual abuse. In fact, the problem may lie not in sexual arousal per se but in social skills. Specifically, some child sex perpetrators are aroused by and desire mutually satisfying relationships with other adults but find it difficult to relate to adult partners (Freund & Blanchard, 1986). If there is some problem with interpersonal skills or social development that makes it difficult for people to engage in relationships with peers, they sometimes target adolescent or younger children because their relative immaturity makes them easier to relate to and manipulate. In this case, sexual development is not the primary problem; the problem lies with social development. Prevention and intervention efforts might need to include at least two approaches: one targeting basic problems with the sexual system and a separate approach targeting relationship skills.

Crucially, developmental psychopathology is concerned with both patterns of maladaption and adaption (Toth & Cicchetti, 2013). Several developmental pathways relevant to child maltreatment have been identified, as shown in Figure 1.3.

Emerging Perspectives

Our understanding of developmental processes that contribute to risk for and response to maltreatment is developing rapidly. Here, we mention a few of the most relevant recent perspectives.

Gene–Environment Interactions

Part of the reason two people can go through similar experiences and come out with different outcomes is that people have genetic propensities that cause them to react to the same situation differently. For example,

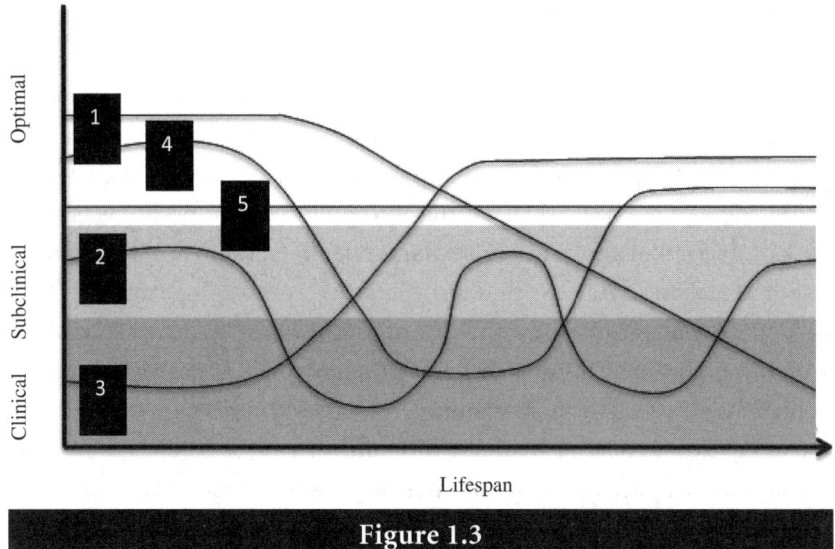

Figure 1.3

After maltreatment, many developmental pathways are possible. (1) Through developmental cascades, a person begins on a path of maladaptation, failing to develop skills in one stage, which leads to further failure in subsequent stages. (2) Although the individual exhibits generally adequate functioning, periods of decreased functioning occur when facing developmental or environmental challenges (e.g., transition to middle school or birth of first child). (3) Generally poor functioning improves when adopted from institutional care or moved from maltreating home to an adoptive home. (4) Generally adequate functioning takes a dip then rebounds (e.g., onset of abuse, then disclosure and support from family or move to foster care). (5) There is generally adequate functioning regardless of environmental stress.

maltreated children with one kind of *MAOA* genotype are more likely to develop mental health problems than are maltreated children with a different *MAOA* genotype (Kim-Cohen et al., 2006).

Epigenetics

Experience can directly affect the expression of genes, so that even identical twins who share the same genes can have very different outcomes depending on environmental experience (Raabe & Spengler, 2013). Environmental factors can lead to changes not in the genome itself but to the epigenome through the presence of tags that affect how genes are replicated and expressed. In several studies, child maltreatment has been shown to alter the epigenome. In one study, people with both posttraumatic stress disorder (PTSD) and a history of maltreatment showed different and more epigenetic changes than did people with PTSD and a history of trauma unrelated to maltreatment (Mehta et al., 2013).

Differential Susceptibility and Biological Sensitivity to Context

Gene–environment interactions may be even more complex that was first thought. It turns out that some genes may be associated with negative outcomes in adverse environments and be associated with positive outcomes in less risky environments (Belsky & Pluess, 2009; Ellis & Boyce, 2008). For example, one genotype is associated with neuroticism among people who were maltreated as children but is associated with openness among people who were not (Grazioplene, DeYoung, Rogosch, & Cicchetti, 2013). In fact, through an epigenetic process, it is possible that some people become more or less influenced by the environment depending on how risky it is. It makes sense that we have both evolved a set of genes that generally promotes survival, and a mechanism to adjust the expression of that genome depending on current conditions. The potential implications of these theories for the study of risk and resilience and ultimately more targeted prevention and intervention strategies for maltreated children are striking.

Experiential Canonalization

Expanding on the gene–environment, epigenetic, and differential susceptibility processes, experiential canonalization is a model that explains how genes and environments jointly influence developmental pathways. In this model, the emphasis is not on deficits in the environment leading to a more or less advantageous outcome. Rather, the emphasis is on how environments and genes work together to influence biology, behavior, cognition, and social relationships in ways that promote adaptation to the environment, with both costs and advantages. Blair and Raver (2012) recently proposed a model explaining how poverty interacts with the stress response system to cause a variety of outcomes. A similar model may explain how some types of maltreatment cause harm.

PLAN OF THE BOOK

The questions before us are important and complex. Answering them requires equally complex scientific models. The good news is that the science of developmental psychopathology can be translated into answers that have a meaningful impact in our communities and families. In this book, we summarize this research and explain how it translates to practice. The Appendix at the end of this book provides an overview of studies that support these findings from a developmental psychopathology perspective.

In the following chapters, we follow a chronological format. In Chapter 2, we look at the maltreatment of infants and toddlers, discussing the long-lasting effects of maltreatment and the difficulties that child protective and public health workers face in evaluating and addressing maltreatment in this highly vulnerable group. In Chapter 3, we focus on preschool children, who have different needs than younger and older children. In Chapter 4, we examine middle childhood, a period in which maltreatment can affect important academic functioning and peer relationships. In Chapter 5, we address the often overlooked problem of maltreatment during adolescence, a period marked by less vulnerability in some ways and greater vulnerability in others. In Chapter 6, we follow major modern developmental psychology textbooks and extend our discussion of maltreatment to effects during emerging adulthood, a period that increasingly requires a variety of supports from families.

At the conclusion of each chapter, a Common Misconceptions section is presented to help dispel some of the myths that are prevalent in the field. We also provide further recommended resources, divided into two categories. More technical resources include scientific journal articles, professional books, and the like for those interested in primary sources. Less technical resources present similar information in forms that are more accessible and tailored for applied settings, such as schools.

RECOMMENDED RESOURCES

Less Technical

Center on the Developing Child, Harvard University. (n.d.). *Interactive features.* Retrieved from http://developingchild.harvard.edu/resources/multimedia/interactive_features
These succinct interactive presentations clearly demonstrate core principles about child development, risk, and resilience.

National Child Traumatic Stress Network. (n.d.). Retrieved from http://www.nctsn.org
This comprehensive site has extensive resources on all aspects of children and trauma for clinicians, researchers, and the community.

Siegel, D., & Hartzell, M. (2003). *Parenting from the inside out: How a deeper self-understanding can help you raise children who thrive.* New York, NY: Penguin.
This accessible book helps parents understand neurobiology, attachment, and how they can parent differently from how they were parented.

More Technical

Goldstein, S., & Brookes, R. B. (Eds.). (2012). *Handbook of resilience in children.* New York, NY: Springer.
This book includes a comprehensive discussion of resilience in general, with specific chapters on maltreatment and trauma.

Lewis, M. & Rudolph, K. D. (Eds.). (2014). *Handbook of developmental psychopathology.* New York, NY: Springer.
This extensive reference book includes a section on trauma disorders and specific chapters on maltreatment, and attachment, posttraumatic stress, and dissociative disorders (Bush & Boyce, 2014).

Siegel, D. J. (2012). *The developing mind: How relationships and the brain interact to shape who we are.* New York, NY: Guilford Press.
This book includes a solid explanation of how brains develop in an interpersonal context over time, how this process can go awry, and how therapeutic interventions help.

2

Infant and Toddler Maltreatment

Maltreatment of very young children is a major concern for child protective and public health workers. The risk of serious injury and death is great for infants and toddlers who are quite dependent on caregivers. A major emphasis in terms of research and clinical work with infants and toddlers has been in basic physical protection of children at risk. Less is known about the long-lasting effects of infant maltreatment on well-being across the lifespan, especially in higher socioeconomic families. It is quite difficult to conduct longitudinal research on maltreated infants through adulthood, and it is difficult for adults to reliably report on maltreatment before age 3 years. Nevertheless, the research we do have points to promising prevention and intervention strategies for this age group. In this chapter, we describe common types of maltreatment among newborns through children aged 3 years, the effects of maltreatment, and some promising interventions for very young children.

http://dx.doi.org/10.1037/14898-002
Child Maltreatment: A Developmental Psychopathology Approach, by K. Becker-Blease and P. K. Kerig
Copyright © 2016 by the American Psychological Association. All rights reserved.

NEGLECT

Neglect is especially common among infants and toddlers and can take many forms (see Figure 2.1). Neglect cases often come to attention of child protective services when parents have difficulty meeting children's basic needs. For example, infants living in a house that lacks heat or food or parents who do not consistently feed their infants and change their diapers, leading to malnutrition and extreme diaper rash, may be discovered and reported to authorities by community members who notice the problem. In other cases, parents fail to protect their children from hazards in the environment. Some examples include infants living in a house infested with insects or rodents or that is extremely untidy, so that there is no clean space for an infant to sleep or eat. Medical neglect is a problem when parents fail to seek medical care for serious acute conditions (e.g., infected diaper rash) or failing to provide care for chronic conditions (e.g., asthma). Neglect can be life threatening. Most maltreatment-related deaths occur before age 3 and are due to neglect (Scannapieco & Connell-Carrick, 2002).

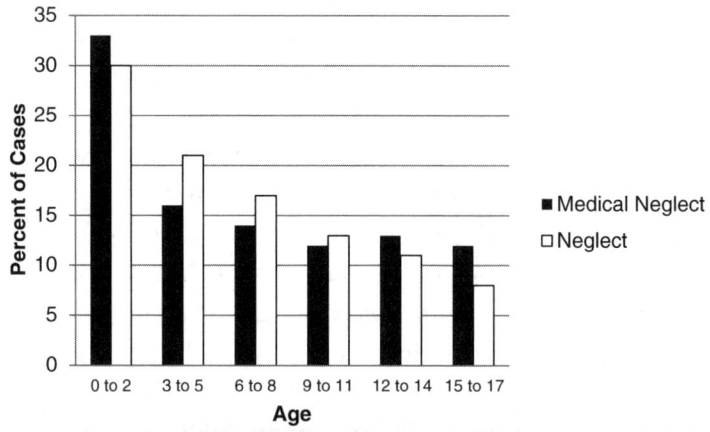

Figure 2.1

One third of all neglect cases involve infants and toddlers. Data from U.S. Department of Health and Human Services, Administration for Children and Families, Administration on Children, Youth and Families, Children's Bureau (2012).

INFANT AND TODDLER MALTREATMENT

Neglect cases tend to be difficult ones for child protective workers. Because of the chronic nature of neglect, it can be difficult to identify and to put effective interventions into place. As one example, here is a case study from a report on a specialized high-risk infants team in Australia:

> On Saturday evening, The Child Protection After Hours Service (AHS) receives a phone call about a 17-year-old woman who has presented at the casualty section of a public hospital requesting assistance for herself and her three-week-old baby. The mother has left her partner after being beaten and has suffered a broken nose and bruising. She presents as being substance affected and admits to consuming alcohol. While waiting for treatment, the mother was observed to allow the baby to roll off her lap onto the floor. The hospital staff do not believe that she is capable of caring for the baby overnight due to the alcohol consumption and the level of her injuries. The baby appears small and thin but is not malnourished and has been checked by a paediatrician and has not sustained any injuries due to being dropped. The AHS Specialist Infant Protective Worker [SIPW] speaks with the mother. She ascertains that the mother is not able to return home and that she is frightened to go to a refuge. The mother's speech is slurred but she is coherent and states that she does not want her baby placed away from her. The AHS is able to find accommodation for the mother at an Adolescent Community Placement (ACP) unit, but the service cannot accept responsibility for monitoring the baby's care. Previously, this situation would have resulted in court action with the child being placed in foster care until a full assessment could be completed. In this instance, the SIPW is able to use the regional HRI [High-Risk Infant Project] flexible budget to secure an agency placement support worker to spend extended periods of time over the weekend with the mother and baby in the ACP. The support worker will monitor the situation and assist in the care of the baby as required. The SIPW is also able to provide funds for emergency clothing and blankets for the baby. As a result of the use of HRI Project resources, the baby and mother are not separated, thereby not interfering with the early stages of bonding and attachment. Also, the SIPW is able to work

cooperatively with the mother concerning immediate planning for herself and the baby which helps to establish a positive tone for the ongoing work that will need to occur with the regional workers. (Naylor, Breen, & Myers, 1999, p. 19)

This case exemplifies the complexity of these cases. It is not clear that the care of this infant reaches the legal definition of neglect, given that the child is not injured or malnourished. The risk of neglect is present but also ambiguous. The mother is young, which is a probabilistic risk factor, but the amount of risk in this particular case is unclear. Substance use complicates the picture, making it unclear whether the mother is temporarily disabled by alcohol use or if there are ongoing concerns. In this situation, who is responsible for the care of the infant? The responsibility for the care of the infant is typically assumed to rest solely with the mother, even in cases like this in which her inability to provide shelter and care for her child are seriously compromised by abuse she has experienced at the hands of her partner. The situation is made worse by the fact that the mother apparently has no friends or family who might temporarily house and care for them. The mother herself is a minor, which leads to the question of her parents' role in protecting her. However, the severity of the situation is attenuated by the fact that a hospital is available and the mother made the decision to seek help there.

In the end, through a program that was specifically designed to respond with flexible solutions to complex cases, this baby was protected, and the mother received the help she requested. As a result, this infant, although at high risk for abuse and neglect, was protected through a creative solution made possible by a special program designed specifically to allow for such flexibility. This example makes it clear that creativity is required to develop, staff, fund, and evaluate effective prevention and intervention programs.

PHYSICAL ABUSE

Physical abuse of very young children is a serious concern in part because their physical size makes them vulnerable. Health records show that the smaller the child, the higher the risk. In one analysis, researchers examined the hospital records of children under age 3 who were hospitalized with a fracture. Doctors judged 12% of those children to have been abused (Leventhal, Martin, & Asnes, 2008). Notably, the percentage of those whose fractures were due to abuse drops over the first 3 years of life, from 25% of infants less than 1 year of age, to 7% of 1-year-olds, and 3% of 2-year-olds. The researchers put the incidence of abuse-related fracture for children under age 1 year at 36.1 per 100,000, considerably higher than the rate for one-year-olds—4.8 per 100,000. Similarly, researchers in Wales examined health records of young children who were not necessarily hospitalized. They found the same pattern of greater vulnerability for babies under 1 year old than for 1-year-olds. They estimated an incidence of 48.3 per 100,000 for 0- to 11-month-olds and 5.6 per 100,000 for 12- to 23-month-olds (Sibert et al., 2002). Together, the data suggest that most fractures in young children are not due to abuse, but abuse-related fractures are more common among young infants.

Fractures are not the only injuries in abused infants. Videotaped evidence of hospitalized infants with their parents show the results of a disturbing variety of physically abusive acts, from poisoning to broken bones to suffocation and strangulation. In an unusual study, Southall, Plunkett, Banks, Falkov, and Samuels (1997) used hidden video cameras in hospital rooms to record the actions of parents suspected of harming 39 children aged 2 to 44 months. In these cases, children with suspicious injuries and illnesses were hospitalized for diagnosis and treatment. While the children were hospitalized, the hospital staff and researchers were able to actually capture video of parents abusing their children in 33 families. Most of the cases involved suffocation, but intentional broken bones and poisoning with hospital cleaning supplies or medication were observed. Even more shocking, the study found that 12 siblings, including infants, of the hospitalized children had already died unexpectedly. This study made it clear that physicians, social workers, and other professionals cannot rely on the self-reports of parents, and hospitalizing and closely covertly supervising families may be one way of detecting serious, hidden abuse among young children.

Infants under 1 year of age are also at risk for inflicted traumatic brain injury. Inflicted brain injury is commonly caused by shaken baby syndrome, which can also result in rib fractures and other injuries. Shaken baby injuries are dangerous and predictable. The incidence rate for inflicted traumatic brain injury among infants under 1 year using the same data set and methodology as described earlier for fractures is lower than for fractures at 27 to 32 per 100,000 (Ellingson, Leventhal, & Weiss, 2008).

Why do caregivers physically abuse infants? There is compelling evidence that infant crying is a trigger. First, the timing of physical abuse matches the typical pattern of infant crying. Abuse-related traumatic brain injury peaks around 3 months of age (R. G. Barr, 2012; Biron & Shelton, 2005; Lee, Barr, Catherine, & Wicks, 2007; Leventhal, Martin, & Asnes, 2010), and abuse-related fractures also typically occur well before children's first birthday (R. G. Barr, 2012; Leventhal et al., 2008, 2010). Accidental falls peak earlier (approximately 2 months of age), and other kinds of accidents are consistently rare (Leventhal et al., 2010). The peak of infant physical abuse closely matches the typical increase and gradual decrease in crying observed in infants between 2 weeks and 3 months of age (R. G. Barr, 2012—see Figure 2.2; R. G. Barr, Trent, & Cross, 2006).

Furthermore, when perpetrators confess to shaking their infants, they frequently report frustration with crying (Adamsbaum, Grabar, Mejean, & Rey-Salmon, 2010; R. G. Barr, 2012; Biron & Shelton, 2005; Starling et al., 2004). In fact, a significant proportion of perpetrators report repeatedly shaking their infants explicitly to stop crying and that doing so stopped the crying. Although we might think of shaking as an isolated incident, in one study, 55% of confessed perpetrators reported an average of 10 shaking episodes (range = 2–30; Adamsbaum et al., 2010). All perpetrators reported that they shook their babies to stop crying, and many reported that the infant would "go to sleep after the shaking" (p. 551). Perpetrators described the events like this: "When I can't calm my son I take him under the arms and, holding him firmly, I move him forward and back.... After I shake him like that, he's tired and goes to sleep" (p. 551). Other reported abusing their infants in fits of rage: "I had fits of anger. She would cry; sometimes, when she did that, I'd shake her.... I was slapping her hard for more than 2 months" (p. 551).

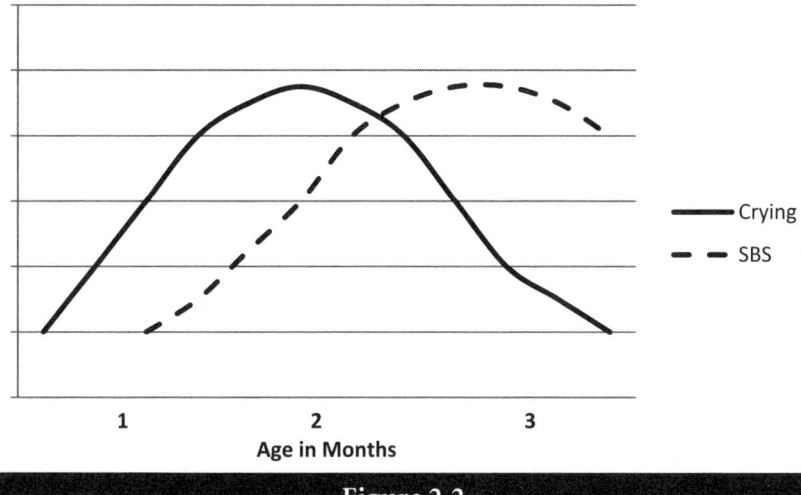

Figure 2.2

Infant crying, followed by shaken baby syndrome (SBS) cases, peaks early the first year of life. Several studies show the same pattern. A few weeks after parents report peak infant crying, hospitals see a peak in shaken baby syndrome cases. Data from R. G. Barr (2012); R. G. Barr et al. (2006); Biron and Shelton (2005); Lee et al. (2007); and Leventhal et al. (2008, 2010).

Notably, perpetrators frequently report a pattern of physically abusive behavior rather than one-time fits of rage. Hospital records also point to patterns of abusive behavior. In one study of shaken baby cases in 11 hospitals over 10 years, 60% of children under 5 years of age who were identified victims of shaken baby syndrome had a previous documented history of maltreatment, and 22% had previous involvement with child protective services (King, MacKay, Sirnick, & the Canadian Shaken Baby Study Group, 2003).

It is impossible to know the true impact of infant physical abuse because so much of it is unreported, and it is correlated with poverty, other types of maltreatment, and other risk factors. However, among recognized cases, approximately 20% of the victims die (King et al., 2003; Starling et al., 2004), and most are impaired at hospital discharge (Starling et al., 2004). Lifelong brain injuries are common (R. G. Barr, 2012). Long-term complications can necessitate the need for complicated and costly medical, child welfare, and special education services.

SEXUAL ABUSE

Limited data indicate that infants and toddlers are at lower risk for sexual abuse. Sexual abuse of very young children comes to light through various means, including children's sexualized behaviors, video evidence of the abuse, perpetrator confessions, and the presence of sexually transmitted diseases and injuries. The American Academy of Pediatrics published guidelines for the medical evaluation of sexual abuse in children, including infants and toddlers. These describe which medical findings are definitive, suggestive, or not indicative of sexual abuse (Kellogg & the American Academy of Pediatrics Committee on Child Abuse and Neglect, 2005).

Both police records and household surveys suggest low levels of sexual abuse among infants and toddlers (Finkelhor, 2007; Snyder, 2000). Some sexual abuse is undoubtedly missed in this age group, but even taking underreporting into account, it is likely that infants and toddlers are at lower risk for sexual abuse than are older children. Nevertheless, infants, including those just weeks old, and toddlers do experience sexual abuse. Girls are more likely to be victims than boys (Cupoli & Sewell, 1988). The prevalence and characteristics of sexual abuse of infants and toddlers are difficult to assess because of the inability for preverbal children to report their experiences and the fact that there is often little or no physical evidence. Some cases are quite serious, with children dying from injuries as a result of sexual penetration (Cupoli & Sewell, 1988; Dubé & Hébert, 1988; U.S. Attorney's Office, 2011).

PSYCHOLOGICAL AND EMOTIONAL ABUSE

From studies of children raised in orphanages, we know that children need human contact, not just food and shelter (e.g., C. A. Nelson et al., 2007). Children who do not receive basic care do not grow well physically or psychologically. However, there is some evidence that young children need even more. It is difficult to study very young children whose basic needs were met and did not experience other forms of abuse or neglect, but did not receive the psychological and emotional care they needed. There are relatively few such cases, and they are difficult to identify. Given the data we do have, it would be ethically problematic not to intervene in such cases as well. Some cases do surface, however. For example, Iwaniec (2006) described a case of a boy adopted from foster care at age 2. When the boy was 4 years old, the parents unexpectedly had a biological child, and soon after had a second child. With the birth of their biological children, both parents continued to provide more than adequate food, shelter, and so forth, but they emotionally withdrew from the boy. They stopped reading to him, playing with him, cuddling and encouraging him. Parenting him was no longer a joy. The boy's behavior changed dramatically. Even more concerning, he lost weight and stopped growing. As his behavior worsened, the parents blamed the boy more and more for "his" problems, and eventually he was moved to a new foster home. It is impossible to know for sure how the boy's early experience before and in foster care interacted with his later care, but his quick decline and failure to thrive when the emotional relationship became neglectful and then blaming suggests that the change in relationship itself caused the child serious physical and emotional harm. Although it remains difficult for legal systems and researchers to establish a definition of psychological and emotional abuse, it is clear that this form of abuse occurs and has lasting influence, even on very young children.

EFFECTS OF INFANT AND TODDLER MALTREATMENT ON DEVELOPMENT

Lack of Care Is Stressful, Especially for Infants and Toddlers

Loneliness and social isolation are stressful for humans of all ages (e.g., Grant, Hamer, & Steptoe, 2009; Hawkley & Cacioppo, 2010). A lack of social interaction and care during the infant and toddler years is especially damaging. During those years, there is no more important developmental task than establishing a trusting, reciprocal relationship with primary caregivers.

Even brief interruptions in reciprocity cause infants distress and activate a stress response. However, brief interruptions are common in well-functioning families. In fact, experiencing some stress during brief interruptions may actually promote growth and resilience. In a classic experiment, infants as young as 3 months interacted with their mothers for 3 minutes. Mothers were then instructed not to interact with their babies and to display a blank (still) face. Babies noticed immediately and begin trying to reengage their caregivers using a surprisingly complex repertoire of behaviors (Brazelton, Tronick, Adamson, Als, & Wise, 1975).

Brief interruptions may cause harm if they occur frequently and without reengagement, but more serious deprivation is devastating. Researchers working from a developmental psychopathology perspective have been interested in clarifying how and why this is so. It has been known for some time that children raised in orphanages have many problems, and the longer children spend in orphanages, the worse the outcomes that can be expected (C. A. Nelson et al., 2007). Although these correlational studies suggested that deprivation caused bad outcomes, researchers could not rule out some other possibilities. For example, it is possible that the children with the most serious problems were most likely to be placed in institutions and to remain there. If so, then early problems may give rise to later problems regardless of where children are raised.

There is now compelling evidence that in fact early institutionalization is the cause of children's difficulties. The Bucharest Early Intervention Project (n.d.) is a uniquely rigorous experiment designed to directly compare institutional care with high-quality foster care (Vanderwert, Marshall, Nelson, Zeanah, & Fox, 2010). Infants who had been abandoned around the time of birth in Bucharest, Romania, and living in institutions were randomly assigned either to continue living in the institution or move to high-quality foster care.[1] Infants moved between 6 and 36 months of age,

---

[1] The ethics of this study were complex. At the time, foster care was not available to infants in Romania, and in fact foster care was not generally regarded as being of higher quality than institutional care; one goal of the study was to provide some clear evidence about which type of care was better to inform Romanian policy going forward. For insight into the ethical challenges of this work and its effects on Romanian children, see Hughes (2013) and Zeanah, Fox, and Nelson (2012).

and on average at 22 months. This design allowed the researchers to test two crucial research questions: (a) Does a lack of care cause harm? (b) Is there a sensitive period during which a lack of care is especially harmful?

The results are compelling and instructive for anyone who works with neglected infants. Children who were moved from institutional care to high-quality foster care had a statistically and practically significant difference in cognitive development by age 42 months. Because the children who were randomly assigned to better quality care did better, there is evidence that it was the lack of care specifically that causes harm.

Furthermore, because the children were moved to foster care at different ages, the authors were able to compare outcomes based on the age at which they moved from institutional to foster care. Within the group moved to foster care, children who remained in institutional care after 24 months, and especially 30 months, had worse cognitive outcomes at age 54 months than did those who moved into higher quality care earlier. By 8 years of age, children who had remained in institutional care longer had more abnormal electroencephalogram brain images than did children who moved earlier (Vanderwert et al., 2010). The evidence suggests that there is a sensitive period; a lack of care that continues beyond 24 months is more damaging than a lack of care earlier in life and of shorter duration.

Lack of Care Reduces Lifelong Resilience

Alan Sroufe helped define the field of developmental psychopathology. He wrote that there are "*three* determinants of behavior and development: genes, environment, and past development" (Sroufe, 2009, p. 180, italics in original). From the beginning, the study of developmental psychopathology has been intertwined with the study of resilience (Garmezy, Masten, Nordstrom, & Ferrarese, 1979; Masten, 2001; Masten & Coatsworth, 1998; Masten & Tellegen, 2012; Masten & Wright, 1998). There have always been some children who flourish in adverse environments. Why? The development of early relationships and the attachment system is part of the answer. When infants receive the reciprocal, sensitive caregiving they need to develop key systems that support attachment, language and cognition, self-regulation, and physical growth, they develop an attachment system that builds resilience for life, whatever life may bring (Bowlby, 1951). As a result, "fostering strong and healthy relationships between children and their caregivers is a key strategy for intervention" (Masten & Coatsworth, 1998, p. 208). Through attachment relationships, children also learn to regulate attention, emotions, and behavior. It is difficult to overemphasize the important of this regulation as a foundation for future academic success, social relationships, and mental health.

When infants are neglected, the attachment system is not functioning well, and the child is at risk. However, the flip side is that those who work with neglected infants and children can increase children's chances of later well-being in at least three ways. First, it is important to look for signs of strength in the attachment relationship between a young child and the primary caregiver. For example, foster parents may find it stressful when young children protest when asked to separate at the end of a visit with a birth parent and worry that this distress is harmful. Viewed another way, this distress may be a sign of a healthy attachment relationship. Like experienced child-care providers, biological parents, and foster parents can help toddlers with separation rather than pathologize children's distress. Second, it is important to look for and nurture any attachment relationships the child might have—for example, with day-care providers, extended family members, and perhaps even older siblings. Children can and do develop multiple attachment relationships with multiple caregivers, and having a secure attachment relationship with one caregiver is beneficial. Third, it is important to support attachment between children and their caregivers. Frequent visitation with birth parents to nurture and sustain attachment even when young children must be placed in foster care is important. In some cases, it may even be possible to provide protection while keeping the young child with their primary caregiver—for example, by placing a teen mother and infant in a foster home designed to mentor the mother as she grows in her capacity to care for the young child.

Maltreatment Affects Children's Emerging Sense of Self

As we have already noted, a key tenet of a developmental psychopathology approach is to start with normative development. Doing so has helped developmental psychopathology researchers better understand how maltreatment affects toddlers specifically. By age 3, normally developing toddlers typically begin to demonstrate a sense of self as measured in multiple ways. Toddlers recognize their own image, can state their own age and gender, use pronouns to refer to themselves, and use words to describe their own internal states. These abilities are markers of young children's emerging sense of self, which they develop over time in relationships with others (Cicchetti, 1991; Sroufe, 1990).

If the ability to understand one's experience becomes more cohesive during these years, we would expect abuse and neglect to affect those abilities specifically. This is just what researchers have found. Maltreated toddlers have been shown to use less language that expresses their internal states (Beeghly & Cicchetti, 1994) and to have a negative emotional reaction when they see themselves in a mirror (Schneider-Rosen & Cicchetti, 1991). P. M. Cole and Putnam (1992) theorized that although very young children are not consciously aware of the betrayal of sexual abuse, the experience would negatively affect a child's basic sense of physical integrity and basic trust in others.

IMPLICATIONS FOR PREVENTION AND INTERVENTION

Nurturing Family-Based Care Can Help Neglected Infants and Toddlers

The Bucharest study findings should give everyone who works with very young neglected children hope and motivation to act early. Early high-quality care changes children's developmental trajectories. The benefits of high-quality caregiving early in life pays dividends by the time young children are kindergarten age and persists at least into middle childhood. This result is in line with the evidence on resilience more generally. What helps children is "ordinary magic": Families who provide consistent, sensitive care for children in their homes really do work magic (Masten, 2014). The foster parents who provide this high-quality care deserve the highest respect and support because the work they do is at once extremely challenging, typically undervalued, and exceptionally powerful.

In sum, neglect affects infants and toddlers through multiple pathways, which explains why the pattern of outcomes is one of multifinality. It produces a stress response that has a range of negative outcomes. Furthermore, it often affects multiple systems that are important for success and well-being throughout lifespan.

Primary Prevention Works to Prevent Shaken Baby Syndrome

Of all kinds of maltreatment, efforts to prevent physical abuse of infants are the most promising. Researchers have identified both a specific period of high risk (2 weeks–4 months of age) and a frequent trigger (frustration with crying). Prevention strategies have targeted new parents with information about the normative peak in crying during the first months of life and strategies for preventing physical abuse (e.g., walking away when feeling overwhelmed). Key components of these interventions are (a) a description of normative crying during early infancy, (b) explaining that shaking a baby is dangerous, and (c) providing examples of what to do when frustrated by a crying baby.

These interventions also target fathers directly and indirectly. In a review of all child abuse deaths of children under the age of 5 in the 1990s in one U.S. state, the most common perpetrators were biological fathers (35%), followed by mother's boyfriends (24%; Schnitzer & Ewigman, 2005). (Mothers were the most common female perpetrator, accounting for 20% of cases.) Some programs have created materials specifically for fathers. One program emphasizes having both parents sign a "commitment statement" indicating their receipt of the materials and that they understood the content (Dias et al., 2005). Another emphasizes that babies often cry more in the early evening, and this has nothing to do with Dad's arrival home from work (M. Barr, n.d.).

Interventions of this type, delivered by nurses in the hospital and through home visiting programs, have demonstrated some success. After implementing a hospital-based educational intervention, rates of inflicted brain injury decreased relative to previous years during a period when no decrease was seen in comparison group (Dias et al., 2005). Interestingly, this change came about even though the vast majority of parents in the study reported that they had previously learned about the dangers of shaking a baby. This finding points to the value of reminding new parents about this danger, even among parents who have already been taught. In a different, randomized controlled trial, mothers reported some change in knowledge about the dangers of shaking babies and increased likelihood of walking away from a crying baby (R. G. Barr, M. Barr, et al., 2009; R. G. Barr, Rivara, et al., 2009). However, there was no difference in parents' frustration level, and in one study, parents in the intervention condition reported greater infant distress (R. G. Barr, Rivara, et al., 2009). Video materials are more effective than brochures, and videos that teach specific behaviors are more effective than videos that are emotionally appealing but do not emphasize behavior change (Russell, Trudeau, & Britner, 2008).

COMMON MISCONCEPTIONS

Misconception: Infants and Toddlers Are Not Affected by Maltreatment Because They Do Not Understand or Remember the Experience

Infants and toddlers may not explicitly recall maltreatment or feel complex emotions such as shame during maltreatment. However, people who experienced early abuse may well feel complex emotions at a later point in development once they understand what happened. More fundamentally, maltreatment affects developing systems necessary for lifelong resilience, as we have described in this chapter.

Misconception: Physical Abuse Is a Greater Threat to Infants and Toddlers Than Is Neglect

Young children, including infants under 1 year old, are at risk for physical abuse. Even so, more very young children are neglected, and die from neglect, than physical abuse.

Misconception: All Stress Is Harmful for Infants and Toddlers

Humans of all ages have an adaptive stress response system. All infants become distressed throughout the day. No parent could always instantly meet an infant's every need. In fact, experiencing distress and then repairing relationships and reorganizing emotional states is beneficial. It is only when infants are left to be distressed for too long without adults to help them recover that stress becomes harmful.

Misconception: Birth to Age 3 Is a Critical Period, and Children Harmed During This Time Frame Will Never Recover

There is some evidence for a sensitive period during very early childhood. However, there is also strong evidence that sensitive, predictable care (e.g., through specialized foster care) is beneficial for young children. In other words, although good-quality care is important for infants, children who do not receive this care can still, in many cases, recover.

Misconception: Young Children Are Naturally Resilient

Some people believe that children are inherently so resilient that they will emerge from early maltreatment without long-term harm naturally, but as this chapter has highlighted, early chronic stress has lifelong consequences, including difficulty with cognition, social relationships, and emotions. Children are highly adaptable, and that can be an advantage, but many children ultimately adapt to harmful circumstances in ways that may not serve them well in the long run. In fact, they may well adapt by creating the appearance that nothing is wrong. In any event, we can give children's "natural" resilience a boost. Early intervention for children who have experienced maltreatment has been shown to help young children.

RECOMMENDED RESOURCES

Less Technical

Center on the Developing Child at Harvard University. (2012). *The science of neglect: The persistent absence of responsive care disrupts the developing brain*

(Working Paper 12). Cambridge, MA: Center on the Developing Child, Harvard University. Retrieved from http://developingchild.harvard.edu/resources/the-science-of-neglect-the-persistent-absence-of-responsive-care-disrupts-the-developing-brain

This science brief describes research findings documenting a typical "serve and return" reciprocal interaction between infants and caregivers and how disruptions in this process during neglect affect very young children.

Cohen, J., Cole, P., & Jaclyn, S. (2011). *A call to action on behalf of maltreated infants and toddlers.* Retrieved from http://www.zerotothree.org/child-development/health-nutrition/childwelfareweb.pdf

This policy brief summarizes the effects of maltreatment and foster care placement on infants and toddlers with profiles of innovative child protection and foster care practices.

Hughes, D. A., & Baylin, J. (2012). *Brain-based parenting: The neuroscience of caregiving for healthy attachment.* New York, NY: Norton.

This book for parents and professionals explains the neuroscience behind healthy attachment and how to promote it.

Zero to Three. (2012). *Safe babies court teams* [DVD].

This short video covers practical, research-based training for professionals who work with infants in foster care. A clip from the video showing the still-face experiment is available at http://main.zerotothree.org/site/PageServer?pagename=ter_stillface

More Technical

Osofsky, J. D. (2004). *Young children and trauma: Intervention and treatment.* New York, NY: Guilford Press.

This important manual summarizes effective interventions for clinicians who work with traumatized young children.

Scheeringa, M. S. (2004). *Diagnostic Infant and Preschool Assessment (DIPA)* (version 7/27/13). Unpublished instrument. Retrieved from http://www.infantinstitute.com

This diagnostic assessment will help clinicians assess the impact of trauma on very young children.

Zeanah, C. H. (Ed.). (2009). *Handbook of infant mental health.* New York, NY: Guilford Press.

This book presents information on risk and resilience, including in the context of parental substance use and violence, applicable to many professionals who work with very young children.

3

Maltreatment of Preschool-Age Children

As toddlers grow into preschoolers, they continue to develop rapidly across many domains. Their growing ability to regulate their emotions, attention, and behavior allows them to take on more complex tasks at school and home. Consistent, responsive caregivers help children develop these skills. Caregivers help children learn to self-soothe, shift between emotional and behavioral states, and label emotions. They also expand children's cognitive understanding of their experiences and the world around them. When preschoolers are abused, their desire to make sense of the situation can, in the absence of support from adults, lead them to make inappropriate causal connections between events, for example, assuming that they are to blame for a parent's angry outbursts. Abused preschoolers are at risk for emotional and behavioral problems that can be severe enough to limit their ability to participate in preschool and community functions, further limiting their opportunities for social and cognitive growth. Developmental psychopathology researchers attempt

http://dx.doi.org/10.1037/14898-003
Child Maltreatment: A Developmental Psychopathology Approach, by K. Becker-Blease and P. K. Kerig
Copyright © 2016 by the American Psychological Association. All rights reserved.

to capture children's cognitive, physical, and social/emotional growth as well as the context in which children develop. In this chapter, we describe common types of maltreatment among preschool children, the effects of maltreatment, and some effective interventions for preschool children.

NEGLECT

Preschoolers are less dependent than infants and toddlers but still at significant risk when parents fail to provide for their basic needs (U.S. Department of Health and Human Services, Administration for Children and Families, Administration on Children, Youth and Families, Children's Bureau, 2012). In a hazardous home, a parent might at least place an infant or toddler in an uncluttered playpen, but it is less possible to restrict an active preschooler from dangers in a hazardous environment. Unlike older children, preschoolers may not have access to free meals at school or at friends' houses.

PHYSICAL ABUSE

Infants and toddlers are at high risk for physical abuse because adults often lack developmentally appropriate expectations about their behavior and injure them in fits of anger. While the challenges of parenting preschoolers differ in important ways, the same underlying factors lead preschoolers to remain at high risk for physical abuse (U.S. Department of Health and Human Services, 2012). In national surveys, the majority of parents indicated that they spank preschool children, and the prevalence rates are higher for preschoolers than for any other age group (Straus & Stewart, 1999). Straus (2000) reviewed evidence that physical abuse is often linked to corporal punishment. Two studies independently showed that approximately two thirds of documented physical abuse incidents were cases of physical discipline that went too far (Gil, 1970; Kadushin, Martin, & McGloin, 1981), and a third study showed that the more physical discipline parents experienced as a child, the more likely they were to physically abuse their own children (Straus, 2001).

Clearly, spanking children is a risk factor for physical abuse as defined by child protection laws. Just as universal, primary prevention strategies have been shown to reduce physical abuse of infants (R. G. Barr, Barr, et al., 2009; R. G. Barr, Rivara, et al., 2009), an analogous effort to prevent spanking universally has been effective in Sweden (Straus, 2005). Those working in this area might start with the same components that made the infant physical abuse interventions successful. Explain what to expect in terms of preschool behavior and preschoolers' limited ability to deliberately manipulate adults. Teach parents how to walk away and calm down when they become angry. Teach parents that spanking has harmful side effects, such as increasing the risk that children hit others. Perhaps most important, tell parents never to spank their children.

SEXUAL ABUSE

Although the risk of physical abuse and neglect does not increase as toddlers grow into preschoolers, the risk of sexual abuse increases substantially (U.S. Department of Health and Human Services, 2012). After infancy and toddlerhood, the reasons why particular age groups experience more or less abuse is complex. Here, we highlight the basics that are most crucial for preventing sexual abuse and understanding the experience of preschoolers who are abused.

Some sex offenders are specifically physically aroused by prepubescent children's bodies. Because of the basic physiological response, pedophiles often have many victims and can be difficult to treat (Hall & Hall, 2007). These pedophiles are a serious threat, but they are not the only threat. Some sex offenders are aroused by both older children and adults as well as younger children. Some are aroused primarily by older children or adults but willing to abuse younger children in certain situations. In one large study, 93% of adult male pedophiles said they were attracted exclusively to children (Abel & Harlow, 2002). This opportunistic pattern of offending may be more driven by the availability and psychological characteristics of victims than a preference for a particular type of victim. Some offenders target preschoolers for their psychological characteristics. Developmentally, preschoolers naturally seek physical comfort from adults they know and trust, are relatively easy to manipulate, and are unlikely to be viewed as reliable reporters.

The American Academy of Pediatrics (Kellogg & the American Academy of Pediatrics Committee on Child Abuse and Neglect, 2005) published specific guidelines for physicians that describe the kinds of physical examinations that are indicated when sexual abuse is performed. In some cases, if the abuse is detected within a few days, physical evidence or injury may be present. However, in many cases, no physical evidence or injury is detectable.

Preschool children are also vulnerable to abuse perpetrated by other juveniles. Peers who have sexual behavior problems, often due to abuse they have experienced themselves, are a risk. Although it is common for preschool-age peers to look at or even touch each other out of curiosity at this age, preschooler sexual behavior that is aggressive and intrusive is abusive and harmful. Preadolescents and adolescents who are sexual with preschool children are also engaged in abusive and harmful behavior. Just as with adult offenders, adolescent juvenile offenders may be motivated by a basic attraction to prepubescent children, drawn toward victims who are easy to manipulate and are unlikely to make good witnesses, or simply because they have the opportunity to access a victim who happens to be preschool age (Hunter, Figueredo, Malamuth, & Becker, 2003; Robertiello & Terry, 2007). Parents and professionals must recognize the diversity among sex offenders; effective prevention and intervention depend on it.

PSYCHOLOGICAL ABUSE

Inconsistent and punitive parenting, even when it does not meet the definition of physical abuse, is psychologically harmful to children (Baumrind, Larzelere, & Owens, 2010; Dodge & Pettit, 2003; Patterson, Reid, & Dishion, 1992; Shaw, Gilliom, Ingoldsby, & Nagin, 2003; Stormshak, Bierman, McMahon, Lengua, & the Conduct Problems Prevention Research Group, 2000). Across many well-designed studies, children of parents who are harsh, rejecting, and punitive during the preschool years (and often continuing later in development) are at increased risk for externalizing, acting-out behaviors both immediately (Stormshak et al., 2000) and later in developmentally, particularly during adolescence (Dodge & Pettit, 2003; Patterson et al., 1992).

Exposure to domestic violence is often considered a form of psychological abuse. Directly seeing and hearing physical abuse can be terrifying and physically dangerous for children. Even children who do not directly witness abuse are affected. The dynamics of abuse often include controlling behaviors, isolation, and family secrecy and shame, all of which can result in children's anxiety, sleep problems, difficulty concentrating, and aggression (Evans, Davies, & DiLillo, 2008; Holt, Buckley, & Whelan, 2008; National Child Traumatic Stress Network, n.d.). Although it is difficult to isolate the effects of exposure to domestic violence in the lives of preschool children who are frequently also exposed to community violence, poverty, child abuse, and other adversity, there is some evidence that domestic violence exposure is associated with posttraumatic stress symptoms in some preschool children. Levendosky, Huth-Bocks, Semel, and Shapiro (2002) studied children aged 3 to 5 living in homes in which domestic violence was occurring. They found that children's posttraumatic stress symptoms were most likely to include talking about the event(s), becoming upset when reminded of the event, increased awareness of what is going on around them after the event, and an unwillingness to separate from the primary caregiver after the event. About a quarter of the sample reported nightmares about the event, replaying the event through violent play, avoiding reminders of the event, or developing new fears. There were no significant differences between those children who directly witnessed abuse and those who were living in homes with domestic violence but whose mothers reported the children did not directly witness it in externalizing, internalizing, or posttraumatic stress disorder (PTSD) symptoms.

EFFECTS OF PRESCHOOL MALTREATMENT ON DEVELOPMENT

Sexual Development

Although it is challenging to research preschool sexual behavior, the evidence suggests two things: (a) sexual behavior is common among preschool children, and (b) some types of sexual behavior are more consistent with a history of sexual abuse than others. The challenge for parents and professionals is to accurately distinguish between common, healthy sexual exploration and less common, unhealthy sexual behavior that may be related to sexual abuse. Some researchers have compared the sexual behavior of preschoolers known to have been sexually abused (Friedrich et al., 2001; Friedrich, Grambsch, Broughton, Kuiper, & Beilke, 1991). Two specific resources are available for clinicians to assess the sexual behavior of preschool children. Preschoolers who have experienced sexual abuse reliably score higher on the Child Sexual Behavior Inventory (Friedrich et al., 2001, 1992). The American Academy of Pediatrics has published a more comprehensive report with a detailed table with a continuum of behaviors and recommended courses of actions (Kellogg & American Academy of Pediatrics Committee on Child Abuse and Neglect, 2005).

Social Relationships

Attachment

According to attachment theory, children develop mental models of themselves and what to expect from caregivers through relationships with caregivers early in life (Ainsworth, 1979; Bowlby, 1969). Attachment styles are a good example of why developmental psychopathology researchers attend not only to genes and environment but also earlier development to predict outcomes. Although toddlerhood is the most sensitive period for the development of attachment, attachment processes are relevant in the preschool period as well (Erickson, Sroufe, & Egeland, 1985; Lyons-Ruth, Alpern, & Repacholi, 1993). In well-functioning families, during the preschool period, Bowlby observed that securely attached children form a partnership with their caregivers, whereby caregivers continue to support children as they explore a wider environment. This exploration during the preschool years is important for learning in and out of school, friendships and other social relationships, and developing increasingly sophisticated strategies for regulating emotions (Crittenden, 1992; Grossmann, Grossmann, Kindler, & Zimmermann, 2008; Moss & Gosselin, 1997; Thompson, 2000).

In maltreating families, children often develop insecure attachment styles with respect to their caregivers. Children who develop insecure attachment styles may tend to avoid seeking care and comfort from adults if they have come to expect that eliciting help from an adult is unlikely to help. Alternatively, they may tend show ambiguous behavior, seeking help from caregivers but also rejecting the caregivers' attempts to respond to their bids. These insecure styles are considered less than ideal but still organized strategies to cope with the environment in which they live. In some models, in fact, these insecure models are considered highly adaptive because they allow children to manage a range of environments, not just above-average ones (Crittenden, 1999). More concerning are disorganized attachment styles that are characterized by a range of contradictory and bizarre behavior that some argue suggest a lack of any organized strategy to obtain caregiving from adults (Solomon & George, 1999; see Crittenden, 1999, for an alternative view).

Preschool children who do not experience consistent and sensitive care from their caregivers sometimes develop a false self in which they display positive affect that does not in fact reflect their true feelings and are compliant to a fault. It is as if they are attempting to manage the attachment relationship with an unpredictable partner by always appearing happy and eager to please (Crittenden & DiLalla, 1988; Main & Solomon, 1990).

Consistent with the hypothesis that maltreatment is associated with disturbances in the attachment relationship that affect children's representations of both themselves and others, Toth, Cicchetti, Macfie, and Emde (1997) assessed the attachment-related representations in preschoolers using a unique approach. The researchers presented the beginnings of stories designed to elicit children's views about relationships and caregiving, had the children finish the stories, and then examined the children's conclusions for indications of their expectations about relationships in general (Bretherton, Ridgeway, & Cassidy, 1990). Using this approach, the researchers found that maltreated preschoolers had more negative representations of both caregivers and themselves.

Social Cognition

Because developmental psychopathology researchers look to normative development to understand pathology, it makes sense that research on maltreated preschoolers includes a focus on social cognition. During the preschool years, children learn to recognize that other people possess different thoughts, desires, perspectives, and beliefs from their own (Flavell, 1999; Wellman, 2002). This understanding is important for the development of empathy and correctly interpreting the motives behind others' behavior. Typically developing, middle-class children begin to understand that different people have different desires (e.g., some children would choose a peanut butter cookie and others a chocolate cookie) around age 2. At age 3, children begin to understand that different people believe different things (e.g., someone who didn't see you put candy in a Band-Aid box would think there are Band-Aids in the box). Children's theory of mind abilities continue to develop into middle childhood (Miller, 2012).

In well-functioning families, most children learn theory of mind through interactions with caregivers over the toddler and preschool years. Beginning around infants' first birthday, caregivers and babies spend time focusing their attention on the same people and objects, for example, through reading books, talking, and playing with toys. These early activities lay the groundwork for more complex social interactions that typically correspond with children's quickly developing ability to understand their own thoughts and the thoughts of others during the preschool years (Tomasello, 1995). For example, skilled parents of 3- and 4-year-olds help children understand their experience, how they feel about their experience, and what others experience and feel. In contrast, abusive and neglectful parents often do not interact with their children in this way (Valentino, Cicchetti, Toth, & Rogosch, 2006). Almost by definition, abusive and neglectful parents do not spend time reading books, talking, and playing with toys. They do not take their children's thoughts, feelings, desires, and beliefs into account or work to share their own perspective in a way their child can understand. As a result, abused and neglected children may not learn as early or as well that different people have different perspectives, and that these perspectives are important to consider in social relationships (Cicchetti & Toth, 1995). At the same time, through equifinality, other children, including many children with autism, fail to develop typical theory of mind abilities despite typical family interaction.

It is, however, possible that some characteristics of maltreatment could actually support preschoolers' theory of mind abilities. Multifinality sometimes leads to opposite outcomes. Open-ended pretend play, for example, is associated with theory of mind. In some neglectful families, it is possible that children are left to play for extended periods and could develop theory of mind skills along the way. Some evidence, largely anecdotal, suggests that lonely children tend to engage in pretend play with imaginary companions, which could in turn be related to theory of mind ability (Taylor, 1999).

Children exposed to violence could have many salient opportunities to learn that others have different thoughts, feelings, beliefs, and desires from their own and have more motivation to infer what others' are thinking and feeling (Pollak, Cicchetti, Hornung, & Reed, 2000). After all, learning to predict and avoid confrontation with an angry, powerful person could be important (Pollak et al., 2000). Some physical and sexual abuse is predictable. On the other hand, many maltreating caregivers are unpredictable. If caregivers behave erratically, children may well learn that it is pointless to try to understand another's perspective (Rogosch, Cicchetti, Shields, & Toth, 1995).

Overall, most of the evidence suggests that maltreated preschoolers' theory of mind skills are less developed than their nonmaltreated peers. Children raised in Romanian orphanages, under conditions of severe deprivation, showed theory of mind deficits that were more severe for youth who spent more than 6 months in care (Colvert et al., 2008). Likewise, Pears and Fisher (2005) found that preschoolers in foster care had worse theory of mind abilities, controlling for intelligence and other factors, compared with low-income children of the same age living with their biological parents. Similarly, Cicchetti, Rogosch, Maughan, Toth, and Bruce (2003) found that maltreated children living with their biological parents showed theory of mind deficits relative to same-age nonmaltreated children. Interestingly, children who experienced maltreatment as toddlers were particularly likely to have poorer theory of mind skills. Together, these findings suggest that a lack of high-quality caregiving interactions during the toddler and preschool years led to difficulty with social cognitive ability, which is typically developing rapidly during the preschool years.

On the other hand, as is often the case with child maltreatment research, it is impossible to rule out other factors, such as prenatal drug and alcohol exposure, peer and sibling experiences, and so forth, that may play a role.

Memory

During the preschool years, children's ability to form and relate coherent narratives about events in their lives develops dramatically. Crucially, this development occurs within the context of conversations with caregivers. Fivush, Berlin, Sales, Mennuti-Washburn, and Cassidy (2003) summarized the process this way: "While young children can remember *what* happened, parent-guided reminiscing helps children to *organize, interpret,* and *evaluate* these experiences in ways that begin to inform children's developing sense of self" (p. 179, emphasis in original).

We know quite a lot about how children learn to relate and remember events in their lives, at least when it comes to discussing positive and relatively benign negative events. In these contexts, by age 3, these children are able to relate past experiences, but they rely heavily on adults who scaffold their accounts by prompting them with questions and generally helping to move the story along. Over the preschool years, they produce more coherent and interesting stories about their lives with less prompting from adults (Fivush, 1994; K. Nelson & Fivush, 2004).

In a series of studies, Fivush and colleagues observed children talking about their lives with caregivers during this time period (Fivush, 1994; Fivush et al., 2003; K. Nelson & Fivush, 2004). Mothers were asked to choose an event to discuss. Depending on the study, it could have been a routine event like a trip to McDonald's, a positive event like a birthday party, or a negative event like a time the child felt sad. From these conversations, Fivush and colleagues learned that preschoolers who develop the ability to tell rich, coherent narratives about their experiences have caregivers who help them elaborate on their memories during the preschool years. Parents who use this elaborative style ask more questions to elicit new information, providing new details for the children to expand on.

We know little about how this process plays out for maltreated children, but there are some important implications to consider. (Developmental psychologists, including Fivush and colleagues, do not typically explicitly exclude maltreated children, but it is reasonable to assume that those parents who are able and choose to participate in these types of studies are relatively unlikely to have maltreated their children.) First, neglectful parents likely fail to have rich conversations with their children. Among physically abused, sexually abused, and neglected preschoolers, neglect is most strongly associated with expressive and receptive language delays, limiting neglected children's ability to participate in rich conversations (Culp et al., 1991). Children whose caregivers tend to ask fewer, less elaborative questions are less able to give detailed, coherent narratives (Fivush, 1994; K. Nelson & Fivush, 2004). By extension, it seems clear that neglected children are unlikely to have the kinds of conversations that would support the development of clear personal event memories. Beyond neglectful parents, it seems unlikely that foster parents would be able to facilitate these kinds of conversations about events that occurred before the foster home placement. Foster parents simply were not there and do not have the same pool of knowledge to use to scaffold these conversations. Furthermore, if the events involve reportable child abuse or neglect, they have likely been advised against engaging in deep conversations out of fear that they could be accused of leading questions that could bias the child's memory for potentially criminal acts. There is a paradox here. These children depend on caregivers to help them make sense of events, but those charged with their care are unable to help them do so.

Second, some parents provide narratives that are self-serving or confusing to children. Physically abusive parents often blame children for the abuse, calling it punishment. Sexually abusive parents likewise tend to tell stories that lead children to believe they were responsible. Parents with mental illness or substance abuse may not have complete memory or have distorted memories that they share with their children. The first author once spoke with a mother about a time when child protective services had removed her children. She said she did not neglect her children. Rather, she chose to live with and homeschool them in a tent that she placed in someone else's pasture for more than a year. She pointed out that many people find camping enjoyable and educational, and this was how she framed the situation for her children.

Third, in some circumstances, caregivers actively silence children's stories, consciously or not (Fivush, 2010). When caregivers, as well as adults in the wider society, do not help children talk about and understand their experiences, their memories are more fragmented. It is harder for them to create a coherent verbal narrative about the experience. This silencing is damaging both in terms of memory coherence and to the process of developing a sense of self. At the same time, parents who do not engage in meaning-making conversations with their children may know, on some level, that it may not be beneficial to try to make sense of painful events that cannot be easily resolved. Sales, Merrill, and Fivush (2013) examined how a group of highly traumatized, African American adolescent girls of low socioeconomic status from the inner city thought about their lives. They found that girls who engaged in more thinking about the meaning of the past were more likely to be depressed than those who thought less. "For individuals facing ongoing challenge, it may be more adaptive to simply move forward and assume one can change the future rather than to try to make sense of a past that may simply be senseless" (Sales et al., 2013, p. 106).

Although some maltreated children do not have coherent conversations with caregivers, some have a different experience. In these families, caregivers do reminisce with their children using an elaborative style. These children develop coherent narratives about their lives with one exception: They do not talk about the abuse with anyone. So rather than having a generally fragmented autobiographical memory, they have a coherent life story for everything except the abuse. In these cases, caregivers may send the message that there is some reason not to talk about the abuse. These children are in a difficult position. They have a coherent life narrative, and any fragmented memories they do have of maltreatment do not fit and in fact likely seem implausible. These children, then, develop a skill that is likely useful in terms of long-term resilience that children who experience consistently neglectful or abusive caregivers do not. However, they may be more likely to struggle with confusing, fragmented memories for maltreatment that are difficult to integrate with the rest of their memories (Freyd, 1996).

Traumatic Stress and Dissociation

The fifth edition of the *Diagnostic and Statistical Manual of Mental Disorders* (*DSM–5*; American Psychiatric Association, 2013) includes, for the first time, a PTSD preschool subtype. Subtypes are rare in the diagnosis of mental health disorders, and as of this writing, no specific preschool criteria appear on the horizon for the *International Classification of Diseases* (*ICD*). More typically, ways that a few criteria might manifest differently in children and clinicians' expertise are specified, and these differences are required to assess whether particular symptoms are present and unusual given a child's developmental level. However, in the case of the PTSD preschool subtype, years of careful evidence with children under age 6, and primarily with children aged 3 to 6, led to the conclusion that PTSD is present but significantly different among young children (Scheeringa, Zeanah, & Cohen, 2011). Just as with older children and adults, preschool children must have symptoms of intrusion (e.g., intrusive memories, traumatic play), avoidance (ongoing efforts to avoid reminders of traumatic events), negative alternations in cognitions or mood (e.g., a belief that "I am bad"), and alternations in arousal and reactivity (e.g., sleep disturbance). In the *DSM–5*, older children and adults must have intrusive thoughts that are "distressing." As discussed earlier in this chapter, children under age 6 sometimes appear neutral or even fake positive emotions, so it is difficult for observers to know how distressed they feel internally, so in the *DSM–5*, the "distressing" criterion was dropped for this age group. Similarly, many of the avoidance and negative alternations in mood criteria are difficult for observers to detect and for preschoolers to self-report. For example, relatively few preschoolers were noted to have symptoms such as "loss of interests" or "inability to recall an important aspect of the event." In the *DSM–5*, older children and adults must have more of these symptoms than do children to be diagnosed with PTSD.

Additionally, the *DSM–5* also includes, for the first time, a dissociative subtype under the PTSD diagnosis. Although children can be diagnosed with either the dissociative subtype of PTSD or a dissociative disorder (e.g., derealization/depersonalization disorder, dissociative identity disorder), no specific criteria for preschool children addressing dissociative symptoms exist in the *DSM*.

Diagnosing dissociative symptoms in preschoolers is difficult because it is so difficult to distinguish between normative dissociation and pathological dissociation in this age group. It is normative for preschool children to have imaginary companions who help them cope with normal childhood stress. Identifying pathological dissociation at this age requires a developmental psychopathology approach. First, the clinician must have a clear understanding of normative preschool thinking and behavior, especially with regard to social behavior and pretend play. From there, dissociative experiences that are more intrusive, bizarre, persecutory, and pervasive can be identified. This takes skill and experience, but several clinical tools, reference books, and trainings are available to a wide range of professionals and skill levels. Two useful measures are the Child Dissociative Checklist (Putnam, Helmers, & Trickett, 1993) and the Imaginary Friends Questionnaire (Silberg, 2013). The International Society for the Study of Trauma and Dissociation (http://www.isst-d.org) has a number of useful clinical practice guidelines, handouts for teachers, videos, and webinars, as well as more extensive trainings for clinicians. Books with more information and clinical examples include *The Child Survivor* (Silberg, 2013), *The Dissociative Child* (Silberg, 1998), and *Dissociation in Children and Adolescents* (Putnam, 1997).

Increasingly, providers in the United States will use *ICD* rather than *DSM* codes for insurance billing (Friedman, 2014). It is unclear how this will affect diagnosis and treatment, but it does appear that clinicians will have to work to make the *ICD* criteria work for children. Clinicians working with children and the fourth edition of the *DSM* were able to document intrusion, hyperarousal, and avoidance symptoms with careful behavioral observation. Whereas adults can report distress related to intrusive thoughts, children lack the capacity to do so. Given children's limited ability to identify emotions, think meta-cognitively, and verbally report their distress, clinicians should consider traumatic play as a type of intrusion among children. This is an important issue for clinicians to continue to monitor and for researchers to address over the coming years.

IMPLICATIONS FOR PREVENTION AND INTERVENTION

Psychotherapy Works for Preschool Children

Trauma-focused cognitive behavioral therapy (TF-CBT)—CBT that has been modified with a focus on trauma symptoms—has been demonstrated to be effective for older children (J. A. Cohen, Deblinger, Mannarino, & Steer, 2004; Deblinger, Mannarino, Cohen, & Steer, 2006), but until recently, it was unclear whether CBT could be effective with preschool-age children who lack the cognitive ability for meta-cognition and hypothetical reasoning. A version of TF-CBT has been shown in randomized clinical trials to be effective with preschool children. Scheeringa, Amaya-Jackson, and Cohen (2002) modified the tasks for preschool children in several ways. For example, therapists allow young children to have a caregiver present during a few initial sessions to settle into the routine of therapy. The content of sessions is also modified in several ways. For example, young children are just learning to talk about and name emotions, and this is taught explicitly in a story form. Other concepts are taught implicitly. For example, children are taught self-soothing strategies with the implicit message that they can control symptoms of anxiety rather than the typical emphasis in CBT for older children and adults on identifying and testing unhelpful anxious thoughts.

Child–Parent Psychotherapy (CPP) is a manualized but play based and less structured approach. CPP has been shown to be effective with maltreated infants and toddlers in random clinical trials. Specifically, CPP treatment helps young children develop higher self-esteem and secure attachment and reduces trauma symptoms and behavior problems (Lieberman, Ghosh Ippen, & Van Horn, 2006; Lieberman, Van Horn, & Ippen, 2005; Toth, Maughan, Manly, Spagnola, & Cicchetti, 2002).

High-Quality Foster Care Helps Children

Multidimensional Treatment Foster Care for Preschoolers aged 3 to 6 (MTFC-P) focuses on training and supporting experienced foster parents who provide consistent and sensitive care with an emphasis on positive reinforcement of behaviors. Compared with traditional foster care, treatment foster care includes intensive training and support for foster parents who actively work toward improving children's emotional and behavioral problems in the home setting. (See Boyd, 2013, for a more complete description of treatment foster care.) In randomized clinical trials comparing preschool children removed from their biological homes because of abuse or neglect (or both) versus traditional or treatment foster care, children in MTFC-P had fewer behavior problems and better stress reactivity and attachment behaviors with caregivers (P. A. Fisher & Kim, 2007; P. A. Fisher, Kim, & Pears, 2009; P. A. Fisher, Stoolmiller, Gunnar, & Burraston, 2007).

COMMON MISCONCEPTIONS

Misconception: Preschoolers Who Masturbate Were Likely Sexually Abused

Many preschoolers have sexual behaviors that are typical for their age and are not proof that a child was sexually abused. However, some behaviors are not typical and are more likely to be associated with sexual abuse (see Table 3.1).

Table 3.1

Examples of Normal and Concerning Preschool Sexual Behaviors

Normal	Less common/concerning	Problematic
Kisses other children or adults	Touches peer/adult sex parts	Puts mouth on sex parts
Views or touches new siblings' genitals	Uses sexual words	Asks others to engage in sex
Undresses in front of others	Asks peers/adults to engage in specific sex acts	Inserts objects in anus/vagina
Few, transient behaviors	Behaviors disruptive to others	Persistent and may be coercive

Misconception: All Cases of Sexual Abuse in Preschoolers Can Be Validated With Physical Evidence

Many sexually abused children have no physical signs of sexual abuse.

Misconception: Preschoolers Move on From Bad Experiences Without Adult Help

Preschoolers' moods are labile; they may seem to be unaffected, because their moods shift quickly. Furthermore, because it is easy to overwhelm preschoolers with more information than they can process, experts often advise caregivers only to talk about trauma if children bring it up. In fact, all young children need adults to talk with them about their experiences to help them make sense of their experiences, even if they do not seem affected by experiences they have had. When legal concerns limit direct caregivers' ability to have conversations about abuse and neglect with children, therapy with a clinician who has forensic training can substitute.

Misconception: Nondirective Play Therapy Is the Only Type of Therapy for Preschool Children

Play therapy that is open-ended and focused on helping children express themselves is not the only option and may not be as effective as other types of therapy. CPP, for example, is play based and supported by a manual to help therapists target specific behaviors and symptoms, and TF-CBT adapted for preschool age children is a more structured approach. Both are supported by rigorous effectiveness research.

RECOMMENDED RESOURCES

Less Technical

Koplow, L. (Ed.). (2007). *Unsmiling faces: How preschools can heal* (2nd ed.). New York, NY: Teachers College Press.
    This practical guide explains how preschool teachers can meet children's social and emotional needs and includes a chapter on traumatized children.

More Technical

The Institute of Infant and Early Childhood Mental Health website. *Measures and manuals.* Retrieved from http://www.infantinstitute.org/measures-manuals
This website has several resources for clinicians working with maltreated and traumatized preschoolers including the Preschool PTSD Treatment Manual (Scheeringa, Amaya-Jackson, & Cohen, 2002).

Leve, L. D., Harold, G. T., Chamberlain, P., Landsverk, J. A., Fisher, P. A., & Vostanis, P. (2012). Practitioner review: Children in foster care—vulnerabilities and evidence-based interventions that promote resilience processes. *Journal of Child Psychology and Psychiatry, 53,* 1197–1211.
The authors summarize effective foster care interventions implemented internationally for preschoolers, as well as younger and older children.

Silberg, J. L. (2013). *The child survivor: Healing developmental trauma and dissociation.* New York, NY: Routledge.
Silberg is a leading authority on treating childhood dissociation. This book is relevant for preschool children as well as older children.

4

Maltreatment in Middle Childhood

Unlike infants, toddlers, and preschoolers, the vast majority of children aged 6 to 12 have one obvious protective factor: Nearly all attend school outside of the home. Schools confer a number of advantages. First, for children who experience maltreatment at home, school is a safer environment. Second, schools provide at least one meal a day. Third, school employees are mandated reporters of abuse and intervene when they notice signs of maltreatment. Fourth, at school, children have the opportunity to engage in social relationships with teachers, administrators, counselors, nurses, and other nurturing adults who socialize and support maltreated children in important ways.

http://dx.doi.org/10.1037/14898-004
Child Maltreatment: A Developmental Psychopathology Approach, by K. Becker-Blease and P. K. Kerig
Copyright © 2016 by the American Psychological Association. All rights reserved.

NEGLECT

In general, school-age children are less vulnerable to neglect than younger children. School-age children are less dependent on caregivers and more active in the community outside their homes. Attentive neighbors, teachers, and friends' parents may be able to provide some caregiving that helps to offset the lack of care at home. There are some important caveats, however. Some parents of neglected children prevent them from leaving home. Others feel responsible for the care of younger siblings and feel obligated to remain at home as much as possible to care for them. Either way, despite the theoretical ability to escape the situation, they may be functionally trapped. School-age children have new developmental needs as well. School-age children need social and emotional support, and they depend on caregivers to help them obtain clothes and supplies, complete homework, and safely get to school. Thus, they are at especially high risk of educational neglect.

PHYSICAL ABUSE

Compared with younger children, fewer school-age children are identified by child protective services as having been physically abused (U.S. Department of Health and Human Services, Administration for Children and Families, Administration on Children, Youth and Families, Children's Bureau, 2012). Risk of homicide declines over the preschool period and increases again beginning in the teenage years, with a trough of particularly low risk between the ages of 5 and 12 (Finkelhor, 2013).

It is likely that school-age children experience physical abuse that is qualitatively different from that experienced by young children. They are at lower risk for serious injury given their growing size. Their advancing social, emotional, and cognitive development makes it easier for them, to some extent, to avoid provoking the same kinds of angry punishments that more impulsive younger children might. However, their ability to physically sustain more violence, and to hide it from others, may translate into quite serious, chronic abuse.

SEXUAL ABUSE

The risk for sexual abuse, unlike the risk for neglect and physical abuse, continues to increase in school-age children (U.S. Department of Health and Human Services, 2012). Most sexual abuse perpetrators of both boys and girls are men (Negriff, Schneiderman, Smith, Schreyer, & Trickett, 2014). Girls are more likely than boys to be sexually abused, and they are more likely to be abused by a family member, whereas boys are more likely to be abused by non–family members (Negriff et al., 2014). Children with disabilities, including behavioral and cognitive disabilities, are at higher than average risk for sexual abuse (U.S. Department of Education, 2004).

It is important to understand how sexual offenders gain access to school-age children, select victims, and groom them to be more compliant and less likely to disclose. Elliott, Browne, and Kilcoyne (1995) interviewed 91 child sex offenders about their crimes. They found that half chose children whom the offenders perceived to lack confidence or have low self-esteem, and almost as many said that a "special relationship" with the child was essential. Said one, "I have to feel as if I am important and special to the child and giving the child the love she needs and isn't getting" (p. 584). Most offenders who targeted children outside their own families had a set repertoire of strategies for gaining the trust of not only the child but often of the child's entire family. The most popular strategy, used by 48%, was to offer to babysit. Once alone with the child, they bathed or dressed the children or coerced them with statements that the sexual activity was normal or had educational value. Although some used force, the most popular strategies included using "accidental" touch and other activities to slowly desensitize children to the abuse, stopping if the children protested.

It is essential that parents, teachers, law enforcement, clinicians, and other adults understand that most children are abused by someone they trusted who took a lot of time and care to develop a special relationship with that child and to systematically confuse them about the nature of the sexual activity. From this perspective, it is less realistic to expect children to be able to detect and deter offenders. Children are dependent on adults for physical and emotional care; they are also immature and simply no match for a manipulative offender. This perspective makes it clear why children often do not disclose the abuse immediately or why they "went along with it." Understanding the process of manipulation makes it harder for perpetrators to claim children instigated the abuse, never seemed upset or said no, or that they were exaggerating.

Although sexual abuse frequently happens in private homes (Elliott et al., 1995), schools are not safe havens for all students. Research on educator abuse within schools is scarce, but the evidence suggests that sexual abuse by educators follows a similar pattern to sexual abuse in general (U.S. Department of Education, 2004). Perpetrators are overwhelmingly male, and tend to target girls. Perpetrators use the same tactics as other perpetrators, looking for vulnerable children who are unlikely to report the abuse or be believed and grooming their victims to make them less likely to identify or report the abuse (U.S. Department of Education, 2004).

Even children who are not direct victims are harmed by the prevalence of sexual abuse in society. Girls at this age can be quite worried about sexual abuse, and their fear is often increased by media coverage of incidents (Becker-Blease, Finkelhor, & Turner, 2008; Tulloch, 2000).

PSYCHOLOGICAL ABUSE

Because physical punishment of children generally declines after age 5, we might predict that psychological aggression would decline as well, but this is not the case. Straus and Field (2003) asked parents how often they did any of the following: (a) shouted, yelled, or screamed at him or her; (b) threatened to spank or hit him or her but did not actually do it; (c) swore or cursed at him or her; (d) said they would send him or her away or kick him or her out of the house; and (e) called him or her dumb or lazy or some other name like that. They considered (a) and (b) (less serious) separately from (c), (d) and (e) (more serious). For children aged 6 to 12, more than 90% of parents reported any psychological aggression, and the rate remains constant through middle childhood. For severe psychological aggression, the rate increases from approximately

30% of parents reporting the more severe behaviors targeting their 6-year-olds up to a peak of 50% for 10-year-olds, at which point the rate holds steady into adolescence. It is difficult to know how much of this psychological aggression reaches a legal or any other threshold of psychological abuse. Marshall (2012) provided a relevant clinician's guide with case studies that helps clinicians and other professionals consider when these behaviors cross the line to abuse and how to best respond.

EFFECTS OF MALTREATMENT

Maltreatment Alters the Timing of Puberty

It is normal for school-age children to begin puberty near the end of elementary school. By the early 1990s, however, clinicians noticed that girls who experience sexual abuse begin puberty earlier (Trickett & Putnam, 1993). Normatively, around age 10 on average, girls' breasts begin to form. Approximately 2 years later, on average, girls begin menstruating. Several studies show that sexually abused girls begin menstruating earlier (Boynton-Jarrett et al., 2013; Chisholm, Quinlivan, Petersen, & Coall, 2005; Herman-Giddens, Sandler, & Friedman, 1988; Turner, Runtz, & Galambos, 1999; Zabin, Emerson, & Rowland, 2005).

Just why sexually abused girls begin menstruation earlier is an area of active research. As a first step, it is important to determine whether there is evidence that premenarche sexual abuse causes girls to begin menstruating earlier, as opposed to the reverse. That is, it is possible that some perpetrators may be attracted to girls who have at least some secondary sex characteristics who are at the same time relatively cognitively and emotional immature. Some perpetrators may find these girls sexually attractive and easier to manipulate than older girls. Although it may well be that some perpetrators select victims in this way, the evidence suggests that this is not the most likely explanation for the association between earlier menarche and sexual abuse. Zabin and colleagues (2005) showed that in a diverse sample of 323 sexually abused women, for the majority of them, the sexual abuse began more than 3 years before menarche. This puts the onset of sexual abuse at least a year before the first signs of puberty.

Some theories have suggested that something about the sexual activity itself—exposure to sexual hormones or pheromones, for example—leads to earlier puberty (Herman-Giddens et al., 1988; Trickett & McBride-Chang, 1995). Some evidence is consistent with this view. For example, Boynton-Jarrett and colleagues (2013) found that the adjusted odds ratio for early menarche (before age 11) increased as the degree of physical contact during the abuse increased.

Perhaps the most dominant theory, however, is that stress, rather than sexual abuse per se, leads to earlier sexual maturation and menarche (Chisholm et al., 2005). From an evolutionary perspective, experiencing a risky environment with low parental support and resources could, at least theoretically, make it adaptive to have children early. In risky environments, parents may die early or otherwise be unable to invest resources into their children. In better times, offspring may benefit when parents have time to mature and gather resources. In risky times, however, parents may not live long enough to realize gains in resources and benefits over time. In those environments, it may be more adaptive for children to be born early. Consistent with the view that parental investment is key, Zabin et al. (2005) found that age of menarche was associated with the relationship between the perpetrator and the child. Girls who reported abuse by a father began menarche at 11.6 years of age, compared with age 12.9 for girls without a history of sexual abuse and age 12.5 for girls who reported abuse by a stranger. Evolutionary theory would explain this finding by speculating that if there is no guarantee of safety, parenting support, or even survival in the future, it may make sense to reproduce quickly rather than wait for better conditions. In contrast, stress is linked with activation of the hypothalamic–pituitary–adrenal axis, which is in turn linked with a suppression of sex hormones and a delay in sexual maturity. In this model, if conditions are poor, it may not make sense to reproduce early.

It is possible for biological and psychosocial stressors and supports to interact in such a way that both of these theories are true under different circumstances (Ellis & Boyce, 2008). Two studies directly test this theory and find support for it. Zabin and colleagues (2005) found that physical abuse was associated with both early and late menarche, and sexual abuse was associated with early menarche. Chisholm and colleagues (2005) found that early childhood stress, including physical violence and insecure attachment, is negatively related to age of menarche and childbearing.

Whatever the cause of early puberty, it generally is not associated with positive outcomes. Girls who begin puberty earlier tend to draw the attention of older youth, which in turn can lead to drug use, precocious sexual activity, and unplanned pregnancy (Flannery, Rowe, & Gulley, 1993). Girls who enter puberty earlier are also at higher risk for eating disorders and depression (Kaltiala-Heino, Kosunen, & Rimpelä, 2003; Kaltiala-Heino, Rimpelä, Rissanen, & Rantanen, 2001).

For researchers, there is much work left to do. The mechanisms through which early puberty leads to delinquency have yet to be fully explicated, especially for youth from various ethnic backgrounds (Cavanagh, 2004).

For clinicians, this work leads to some important developmental considerations. Because children who begin puberty early are statistically at increased risk for mental health and other problems during adolescence, and clinicians may be able to help prevent or intervene early by working with early maturing girls before the onset of full mental health disorders. Knowing about this developmental pathway may help clinicians and caregivers empathize with early-maturing girls. They may well be put into situations involving substance use and sexuality before they are cognitively ready or before adults have provided guidance and education. In this case, attending to pubertal timing may be more clinically useful than attending to chronological age.

Dissociation Can Interfere With the Development of Self-Regulation

School-age children are increasingly able to regulate attention, emotions, and behavior. Their increasing capacity for self-regulation allows children to grow academically and socially. In contrast, maltreated children often have difficulty regulating attention, emotions, and behavior. For some children, the lack of normally expected growth in self-regulation is due to dissociation.

Dissociation is defined as a lack of integration of thoughts, feelings, and behaviors that are normally expected to be integrated. Putnam (1997), through the discrete behavioral state theory, explained dissociation in terms of a lack of integration of behavioral states that are normally not integrated at birth but become integrated over the first years of life. Infants normally spend their time in deep sleep, REM sleep, crying, fussy, quiet-alert, and active-alert states (Wolff, 1987). Caregivers help infants move between states—for example, by rocking a fussy baby to sleep. Over time, children gain more states, an awareness of states other than the current state, and the ability to move between states independently. Neglected children are left to cope with distressing states alone, which is a stressful experience for young children. Abused infants can experience extreme states of fear that are difficult to integrate with other experiences. As a result, children may enter a state of extreme fear and get "stuck"—that is, unable to see that other states are possible or shift out of a fearful state. Instead of developing a coherent sense of self that exists even as the person experiences different states, some maltreated children, especially those who experience early and chronic maltreatment, experience clusters of state-dependent thoughts, emotions, and behaviors. Over time, in the most extreme cases, some come to experience these different clusters of states as different identities. Dissociation is best considered along a continuum with the degree of awareness between states varying from total to none, and most dissociative children experience some awareness that may be fragmented or incomplete.

Silberg (2013) extended Putnam's theory, among others, and presented a model for working with children who experience a range of dissociative experiences.

Attention Dysregulation Is a Problem for Many Maltreated Children

Several studies have shown an association between attention-deficit/hyperactivity disorder (ADHD) and maltreatment in samples of children seen at community, hospital clinic, and community clinic settings (e.g., Becker-Blease & Freyd, 2008; Briscoe-Smith & Hinshaw, 2006; Ford et al., 2000; Glod & Teicher, 1996; Leslie, Stallone, Weckerly, McDaniel, & Monn, 2006; Weinstein, Staffelbach, & Biaggio, 2000).

The causes of attention problems generally and ADHD specifically are multifactorial (Nigg, 2010; Richards, 2013). Difficulty concentrating and erratic behavior can be caused by dissociation or posttraumatic stress disorder (PTSD) but resemble ADHD. Even low levels of lead exposure can produce ADHD symptoms (Nigg, 2010), and it is possible that maltreated children are at increased risk for lead exposure. It is also possible that the presence of family members (adults, children, or both) with PTSD is a risk factor for child maltreatment for a variety of reasons (Mulsow, O'Neal, & Murry, 2001).

Despite theoretical and empirical evidence that suggests child maltreatment may be an important factor to consider when designing interventions for children with ADHD, research on maltreatment tends to be published in journals and presented at conferences outside of the mainstream clinical field. As a result of these silos, many clinical interventions are inadequately informed by research on maltreatment. The most comprehensive study on the treatment of ADHD among school-age children explicitly excluded children with ongoing or unreported abuse (MTA Cooperative Group, 1999). Implicitly, many children experiencing parental substance abuse, educational neglect, and poverty were also effectively excluded: Further exclusion criteria included children who were absent one quarter or more of the school days in the past 2 months, had a parent who abused stimulants, had no telephone, or had changed caregivers within the past 6 months. The reason for excluding these children, in general, was a lack of confidence that they or their parent would be able to participate in the treatment. As a result, we simply do not know whether the treatments that are effective for most children are effective for maltreated children, and we do not have good alternatives for families who are unlikely to benefit from existing treatment.

Unfortunately, the lack of awareness of possible maltreatment in the lives of children with attention, hyperactive, and impulsivity problems extends to mental health professionals. Overmeyer, Taylor, Blanz, and Schmidt (1999) asked clinicians to evaluate children who had been diagnosed with hyperkinetic disorder using the *International Classification of Diseases*, 10th revision. In some cases, the evaluators knew the child's diagnosis, and in other cases they were blind to it. When clinicians knew the child's diagnosis, they were less likely to note a range of negative interactions in the family and were specifically less likely to ask about or identify the presence of physical abuse in the family.

The take-home message for mental health professionals is that attention, hyperactivity, and impulsivity problems are prevalent among maltreated children, and maltreatment is prevalent among children with these problems (e.g., Becker-Blease & Freyd, 2008; Briscoe-Smith & Hinshaw, 2006; Ford et al., 2000; Glod & Teicher, 1996; Leslie et al., 2006; Weinstein et al., 2000). Mental health professionals must educate themselves on the possible links between maltreatment and ADHD and the best possible treatment approaches for maltreated children rather than solely rely on standard guidelines.

School Engagement Predicts Academic Success

Maltreated children often struggle academically (S. F. Cole, Greenwald O'Brien, Gadd, Ristuccia, Wallace, & Gregory, 2005), but so do many other children. This is a classic case of *equifinality*: Many factors lead to the same outcome. Because there are many reasons why children struggle at school, it is important for researchers and mental health clinicians to carefully evaluate multiple developmental pathways, including those that involve social, academic, and other concerns.

School engagement is a relevant factor to consider both because it is a powerful predictor of school success and a potential target for intervention. Shonk and Cicchetti (2001) examined maltreatment, school engagement, and academic maladjustment in a sample of low-income children known to child protective services. Teachers rated children's effort and ability in their classrooms. To assess academic maladjustment, researchers looked for evidence of being retained a year in school, excessive absences, special education services, suspension, and low achievement test scores. In this study, a maltreatment history predicted lower school engagement, which in turn predicted more academic maladjustment.

In a sample of foster children, Pears, Kim, Fisher, and Yoerger (2013) examined multiple types of school engagement—behavioral (physical attendance), affective (enjoyment and feelings of connection), and cognitive (effort spent on academic tasks). The researchers found that maltreated children in foster care experienced less affective and cognitive engagement in kindergarten, which in turn was related to lower academic ability in late elementary school.

Mental Health Professionals Can Help Siblings Bond in Foster Care

A minority of maltreated children spend significant time during middle childhood in foster care. Although those who remain in foster care are a relatively small group, clinicians and other professionals are frequently consulted about the best living situations, therapies, school plans, and so forth that will meet these children's diverse needs. For foster youth, maintaining bonds is an important issue. Having lost their parents, the threat of losing the rest of their birth family is doubly difficult. Given how important this issue is to foster youth, as well as caseworkers and biological parents, it is surprising that more research is not available to help make good placement decisions (Kothari et al., 2014).

The Children's Bureau (Child Welfare Information Gateway, 2013b) provided a solid research summary of what is known about the placement of siblings when two or more need to be placed in foster care. Although many of their recommendations target child welfare policies and practices, some recommendations are specifically relevant for mental health professionals. Specifically, the authors highlighted the influential role mental health professionals' clinical judgments have in making sibling placement decisions. Following are some key judgments clinicians make, along with a discussion of relevant research and issues for mental health professionals.

- "There is too much conflict or rivalry between particular siblings to keep them together."

Conflict between siblings related to problems for foster care should not be ignored (Linares, Li, Shrout, Brody, & Pettit, 2007). However, clinical psychologists may well be able to reduce sibling conflict if they are made aware of the problem. A clinical psychologist may not independently rank sibling conflict among the most pressing problems to address but may be able to reduce sibling conflict through effective interventions if made aware that the conflict is a significant problem for the foster parents.

- "A single child with special needs requires a separate placement."

Often, one sibling has chronic physical or mental health needs that are stressful and strain the family's resources. Mental health professionals may not be aware of the extent of the stress this causes or the likelihood that the stress could result in a disrupted placement. After all, mental health professionals who treat families outside of the foster care system are unlikely to see parents who are considering excluding a child from their home, even if the child's needs are extremely stressful. Mental health professionals can help parents cope with the stress of a child's chronic medical problem, whereas medical professionals treat the problem itself. Mental health professionals can also directly treat mental health symptoms, starting with those that are most disruptive. A mental health professional may also be in the best position to determine whether a different, perhaps temporary, placement is necessary.

- "An older child is too involved in taking care of a younger brother or sister."

This situation is both tricky and common. On the one hand, the older sibling may well be a major attachment figure and source of support for younger siblings (Child Welfare Information Gateway, 2013b). On the other hand, an older child who has been put in the position of acting as a parent may be at significant risk. These children do not have the chance to master developmentally salient tasks, and too much of their time and resources is shifted away from learning important skills and knowledge toward caring for younger siblings. At the same time, younger siblings tend to continue to look to the sibling, rather than the foster parents, to get their needs met, and the pattern can be difficult to break. At the same time, the presence of this pattern does not mean de facto that the sibling group must be separated. It is possible with family and individual therapy to retain the bond between siblings while working toward a more developmentally appropriate relationship.

- "A sibling born after older siblings have been removed from the home can be considered separately for purposes of permanency goals because the children do not have an established relationship."

There is certain logic to this principle. If siblings have an established relationship, particularly if it is positive, there is reason to support that relationship. However, the presence of a relationship is not necessary to work toward placing siblings together. Long after siblings exit foster care, they will at least have a connection by blood with their sibling, and nurturing that relationship during childhood could provide an important lifelong source of support.

The overriding principle is that mental health professionals who are asked to make recommendations about the best interests of children should carefully consider the risks and benefits associated with placing siblings together. They should also consider the effects of overriding siblings' expressed desire to be together and the possibility of providing services that could attenuate concerns while supporting the benefits of placement together. Even if placement in the same physical location is not possible, they can help child grieve the loss of a sibling relationship and encourage whatever kind of relationship is possible through visits and communication.

In sum, there are many ways in which mental health professionals can help siblings remain in the same home or to maintain a relationship. There remain cases, however, in which separation is best (Hindle, 2000). In some cases, for example, siblings have perpetrated abuse against a sibling, and placing the children together poses ongoing risk to the victim. Hindle (2000) provided a clinical overview of the relevant issues, along with case examples.

IMPLICATIONS FOR INTERVENTION AND PREVENTION

Cognitive Behavioral Therapy Helps School-Age Children

Two adaptations of cognitive behavioral therapy (CBT) are especially relevant for maltreated school-age children: trauma-focused CBT (TF-CBT; J. A. Cohen, Mannarino, & Deblinger, 2012; TF-CBT Web, 2005) and a family-based approach to CBT called Alternatives for Families CBT (AF-CBT; Child Welfare Information Gateway, 2013a). With sessions for both school-age children and their parents, TF-CBT targets trauma-specific cognitions (e.g., "I caused this to happen to me") and behaviors (e.g., avoiding traumatic reminders) using a skills-based approach. The therapy is manualized with room for flexibility depending on children's developmental level, experiences, and symptoms. A well-organized website provides basic training in TF-CBT to those who already have at least minimal graduate training in mental health. TF-CBT has been shown to reduce children's PTSD symptoms, depression symptoms, behavior problems, shame, and negative abuse-related thoughts. Distress among parents of traumatized children was reduced as well (J. A. Cohen, Deblinger, Mannarino, & Steer, 2004; Deblinger, Mannarino, Cohen, & Steer, 2006).

Alternatives for Families cognitive behavioral therapy (AF-CBT) is a family-based approach for families in which physical abuse is a concern or school-age children have behavior problems. AF-CBT is designed to engage high-risk families in a process of education and skill building using a structured approach that is adapted based on family needs. AF-CBT is a promising program that has been shown to reduce both parent and child aggression, child anxiety, family conflict, and risk of harm to children (Child Welfare Information Gateway, 2013a).

Trauma-Sensitive Schools Can Help Maltreated Children Succeed

The needs of maltreated children may seem overwhelming to school teachers and administrators. Fortunately, there are some successful models in two states. Throughout Washington and Massachusetts, teachers and principals have been trained to understand how complex trauma affects learning, and this training has resulted in schools that are sensitive to needs of children who have experienced trauma including maltreatment (Trauma and Learning Policy Initiative, n.d.; Washington State University Extension, n.d.).

Trauma-sensitive schools do not all follow a prescribed curriculum or treatment plan. They also do not offer only specialized trauma-focused services just for traumatized children. Rather, trauma-sensitive schools work with the entire school or district to make all faculty and staff more aware of the prevalence and nature of traumatic experiences children experience and how trauma affects children's learning and engagement at school.

For example, most schools use some exclusion from school (i.e., out of school suspension or expulsion) as a behavior management tool. Suspending children who have experienced trauma, and particularly child abuse, is problematic, however. First, many of these children already have been rejected outright, experienced inconsistent care, or experienced care only when they behaved in certain acceptable ways. Children who cannot depend on caregivers to care for them unconditionally may be harmed when they are excluded by adults at school. They may well interpret exclusion not as a "time-out" to cool off but as rejection and a sign that no adults are consistently caring and supportive. In addition, there is the real question of whether children are better off or even safe when they are excluded from school and expected to stay at home. Trauma-sensitive schools look for alternatives that still meet the children's needs, including the needs of other children in the class who must be safe and able to learn at school. In-school suspension is one option. There, while the student is excluded from class, there is a possibility of an informed staff member working on social or problem-solving skills that may prevent future problems.

Traumatized Children Need Help Learning to Manage Emotions and Behavior

Some approaches to working with children with challenging behaviors operate from the premise that children will behave if they want to, and the goal is to find a way to motivate them to want to comply. Another approach is to assume that children want to meet adults' expectations, but they lack the skills to do so (Greene, 2014). Because maltreated children are especially likely to lack the skills required to function well in families and schools, a good evaluation of exactly what problems they experience and what skills may be lagging is warranted. Mental health professionals with training in maltreatment, trauma, and developmental psychopathology can help biological parents, foster parents, caseworkers, and teachers to understand more clearly what might help a particular child.

Similarly, sexually abused girls too often face a triple whammy: early and inappropriate introduction to sexuality, a lack of sensitive and consistent care and guidance, and early puberty that draws the attention of older boys. When these girls get into trouble with drugs, alcohol, sexuality, and unplanned pregnancy, it can be tempting to judge and punish the behavior. Mental health professionals who look closely at the impact of abuse and neglect and peer group dynamics may need to find new and more effective ways to work with these girls.

Finally, some maltreated children experience dissociation that often goes undetected. They often appear not to be paying attention, noncompliant, or aggressive, but they do not respond to typical interventions. Mental health professionals with some training in dissociation can help parents, caseworkers, and teachers develop more effective strategies for working with dissociative children.

COMMON MISCONCEPTIONS

Misconception: Maltreated Children Mostly Need More Limit-Setting and Structure

Many maltreated children live in chaotic homes, and many have difficulty managing their behavior. It is common to hear social workers and foster parents talk about the importance of firm limits and structure. Clearly, predictable parenting helps maltreated kids (P. A. Fisher, Chamberlain, & Leve, 2009). It is equally important to remember that many maltreated children come from overly structured, rigid homes with too many harsh consequences. Through zero-tolerance policies for misbehavior at school and overly rigid sets of consequences at home can backfire. Routines, limits, and structure works, but only when adults take the time to develop relationships with children and to understand their needs and abilities so that the rules make sense and children can develop the skills necessary to meet adults' expectations.

Misconception: Siblings Always Belong Together in Foster Care

Child protection laws, policies, or recommendations may require siblings to be placed together, and that may be the most desirable outcome—when this is possible. One size does not fit all. Children in care deserve a careful decision based on the risks and benefits for the individual children involved that includes the perspectives of the siblings themselves (Hindle, 2000).

RECOMMENDED RESOURCES

Less Technical

Cole, S. F., Eisner, A., Gregory, M., & Ristuccia, J. (2013). *Helping traumatized children learn: Volume 2. Creating and advocating for trauma-sensitive schools.* Boston, MA: Massachusetts Advocates for Children, Trauma and Learning Policy Initiative.

Cole, S. F., Greenwald O'Brien, J., Gadd, M. G., Ristuccia, J., Wallace, D. L., & Gregory, M. (2005). *Helping traumatized children learn: Volume 1. A report and policy agenda.* Boston, MA: Massachusetts Advocates for Children, Trauma and Learning Policy Initiative.

These books are especially useful for teachers and principals who are interested in understanding the effects of maltreatment and trauma on kids and specific strategies to help them learn at school.

Greene, R. W. (2014). *The explosive child: A new approach for understanding and parenting easily frustrated, chronically inflexible children.* New York, NY: HarperCollins.

Written for parents and useful for teachers and others who work with children, this book describes an approach for working with children with challenging behavior with an emphasis on identifying problems and teaching skills. See also the author's website at http://www.cpsconnection.com.

Schwimmer, D., Quivers, R., Mark McGwire Foundation for Children, Discovery Health Channel (Producers), Roth, V., & Dickson, A. (Directors). (2002). *Close to home.* United States: Direct Cinema Ltd.

The documentary contains some compelling interviews with survivors of child sexual abuse, including a forensic interview with a school-age girl and interviews with child sex offenders.

More Technical

Kothari, B. H., McBeath, B., Lamson-Siu, E., Webb, S. J., Sorenson, P., Bowen, H., ... Bank, L. (2014). Development and feasibility of a sibling intervention for youth in foster care. *Evaluation and Program Planning, 47,* 91–99.

Kothari et al. describe the initial stages of setting up an intervention for siblings in foster care through child protective services, including factors related to feasibility and cost.

Silberg, J. L. (2013). *The child survivor: Healing developmental trauma and dissociation.* New York, NY: Routledge.

This book will help mental health professionals understand the effects of trauma and maltreatment, especially dissociation. It includes an appendix with several useful clinical tools to assess and treat dissociative children of all ages.

TF-CBT Web. (2005). *TF-CBT Web. A web-based learning course for trauma-focused cognitive-behavioral therapy.*

This website provides good basic training in TF-CBT, through clear written information and video vignettes, for professionals with some graduate training in mental health.

5

Maltreatment in Adolescence

Adolescence is a time of risk that ushers in a number of new challenges for the development of youth who have experienced maltreatment. Normative stage-salient issues associated with this period of life include dramatic hormonal changes, the development of sexuality, experimentation with risky behaviors, deepening intensity of emotional attachments to age-mates, the search for identity and sense of self, and the renegotiation of relationships with parents and caregivers to allow autonomy and independence while maintaining a sense of connectedness to the "secure base" of the family (Kerig, Ludlow, & Wenar, 2012; Kerig & Schulz, 2012). All of these are confounding for youth whose developmental course has been set awry by maltreatment or neglect.

Indeed, there is compelling research to suggest that maltreatment that begins or extends into the adolescent years has particularly negative associations with youth adjustment (Ireland, Smith, & Thornberry, 2002;

http://dx.doi.org/10.1037/14898-005
Child Maltreatment: A Developmental Psychopathology Approach, by K. Becker-Blease and P. K. Kerig
Copyright © 2016 by the American Psychological Association. All rights reserved.

Stewart, Livingston, & Dennison, 2008). For example, youth who have reached adolescence when they first come to the attention of child welfare authorities are at higher risk of entering into delinquency (Ireland et al., 2002) and for continuing on an antisocial pathway (J. P. Ryan, Williams, & Courtney, 2013) than those referred earlier in life. A number of hypotheses have been proposed to help explain why the timing of maltreatment matters in adolescent maladjustment. For example, Stewart and colleagues (2008) suggested that adolescence represents a time of particular vulnerability because of the additional stresses and developmental challenges associated with this phase of life. Youth who endure the additional burden of maltreatment while attempting to navigate the difficult transitions of this stage may experience disruptions in important sources of resilience, such as academic functioning and peer relationships, which in turn increase their risk of antisocial behavior and delinquency. In contrast, Smith, Thornberry, and Ireland (2004) proposed that younger children may be more "developmentally resilient" than adolescents: Whereas the short-term negative effects of abuse and neglect may resolve fairly quickly once younger children receive treatment, it may be that interventions are less available and less effective for adolescents.

A different argument was posed by J. P. Ryan and colleagues (2013), who offered that maltreatment in adolescence is in fact a different entity from childhood maltreatment, and one that has more negative implications for development. This, they argued, is because the kinds of parental mistreatment that would draw the attention of authorities need to be more overt and severe in the case of an adolescent than a younger child. For example, in the case of physical abuse, the strength of a blow that would result in an injury requiring medical attention or leaving a lasting mark would need to be significantly greater if the victim were a teenager versus a toddler. Furthermore, J. P. Ryan and colleagues pointed out that when adolescents are mistreated, there may be a tendency for others to view youth as having agency or being implicated in causing the problem. As these authors stated, "at the agency level, social service systems . . . respond . . . differently, as young children are often viewed as troubled and older children are more often viewed as troublesome" (p. 462). Support for their theory comes from a large database following maltreated youth in Los Angeles who subsequently became involved in the juvenile justice system, a group termed *crossover* youth (Herz, Ryan, & Bilchik, 2010). Those youth whose gateway to the juvenile justice system was through the child welfare system were more harshly treated in that they were more likely than their peers to be sent to correctional institutions rather than being put on probation, a difference that held even after controlling for the seriousness of their offenses. Therefore, the advanced developmental status of adolescence may confer risk if others view them as being "problem kids" or in some way complicit in bringing about the violence in their lives.

ADOLESCENCE BRINGS NEW SOURCES OF RESILIENCE

On the other hand, the adolescent stage also brings with it a number of potential sources of resilience. Brain development progresses and, although not yet complete, the structures associated with executive functions, self-control, and complex reasoning mature. The widening and deepening of social networks means that adolescents from maltreating homes may have options for turning to extrafamilial sources of instrumental and moral support (e.g., coaches, mentors, spiritual leaders, friends' parents) that are not as accessible to younger children. Furthermore, adolescents increasingly are in their own "driver's seats," quite literally, as they gain more of the mobility and means to make choices regarding their own physical, mental, and emotional environments.

MULTIPLE DEVELOPMENTAL PATHWAYS EMERGE DURING ADOLESCENCE

Another complication that arises is that, for some adolescents, maltreatment during the teenager years is a continuation of a long history of abuse dating back to earlier periods and thus the effects are cumulative and cascading across these different developmental phases. However, for other adolescents, maltreatment begins in this period, perhaps instigated by the increasing levels of challenging behaviors and parent–child conflict that are frequently seen among teenagers. Interestingly, some research suggests that it is maltreatment that begins early in life and continues into adolescence that has the most negative effects, particularly in regard to the development of antisocial behavior (J. P. Ryan et al., 2013; Stewart et al., 2008). Where the literature allows us to chart the differences between youth with these different developmental trajectories of maltreatment, we will do so; however, a caveat is that not all of the studies examining the effects of abuse on adolescent development are careful to make this distinction between childhood versus adolescent onset.

In addition, as we have discussed in other developmental periods, the majority of adolescents who experience maltreatment do so in multiple ways; in fact, the likelihood of polyvictimization increases with age (Dierkhising et al., 2013). Thus, it is not surprising that much of the research on adolescent abuse identifies youth as "maltreated" or combines forms of maltreatment rather than distinguishing between specific effects associated with neglect or physical, sexual, or emotional abuse.

NEGLECT

Although most of the attention in the literature on neglect has focused on younger children, adolescents too can be the victims of parental neglect. In fact, in a recent review of the available data, Trickett, Negriff, Ji, and Peckins (2011) found that overall incidence rates for neglect in the United States were highest in the early adolescent years compared with any other period (9.1 youths per 1,000). Moreover, some research suggests that the effects of neglect are particularly negative when the child concerned is a teenager. As noted earlier, one theory offered as to why this might be so is that the forms of parental neglect that are serious enough to capture the attention of child protection agencies when youth are in their teens are particularly harsh and damaging (J. P. Ryan et al., 2013). For example, whereas neglect of a younger child might be seen in an unkempt home and an unstocked refrigerator, neglect of an adolescent might take the form of a parent locking the child out of the house or failing to provide protection from a sexual predator. Thus, neglect in the younger years might comprise an act of omission (i.e., failing to provide nurturance or care), whereas neglect in adolescence may be better characterized as an act of commission (e.g., purposefully taking away resources needed for a youth's emotional or physical safety).

However, there are compelling data to suggest that neglect in early childhood casts a long and malevolent shadow that extends into adolescence. For example, findings from the longitudinal Minnesota Mother–Child project (L. A. Sroufe, Egeland, Carlson, & Collins, 2005) showed that among participants subjected to various forms of maltreatment in early childhood, neglect was associated with the worst outcomes later in life, including a wide range of adolescent academic, social, behavioral, and emotional problems. Adolescents who were victims of early neglect were the most likely to engage in delinquent behaviors, substance abuse, and school dropout; were more aggressive; and were more likely to have made a suicide attempt. Strikingly, although all forms of maltreatment increased the risk for a psychiatric diagnosis, the highest rates were for neglect: In this sample, only one of the youth who had experienced early neglect had not received a psychiatric diagnosis by age 17. Consistent with a developmental psychopathology model, these data are suggestive of the ways in which the lack of an early "average expectable environment" (Cicchetti & Valentino, 2006) can interfere with the successful navigation of subsequent stage-salient issues in ways that cascade across developmental periods and culminate in adolescent maladaptation.

SEXUAL ABUSE

Although many of the studies on maltreatment combine forms of abuse, as noted earlier, there is an important body of research devoted to the specific effects of sexual abuse on adolescents. And for good reason: National surveys such as those conducted by Finkelhor, Turner, Ormrod, and Hamby (2009) indicate that the peak period of vulnerability for sexual victimization is age 15. Although norms regarding what is appropriate regarding sexual contact between children and adults may vary across cultures, cross-cultural definitions of sexual abuse concur that this involves sexual activity that the youth does not comprehend, is unable to give consent to, is developmentally unprepared for, or that violates the laws and social mores of the community (World Health Organization, 2010). With this in mind, global data from the World Health Organization (2010) indicate that an estimated 150 million girls and 73 million boys under age 18 have experienced some form of sexual maltreatment at some time in their lives.

Furthermore, there are striking gender differences in the prevalence of sexual abuse, with girls 3 times more likely than boys to be victims and the gender ratio growing with age: Although the ratio of girls to boys is 2:1 in infancy and 3:1 in middle childhood, it increases to 6:1 in adolescence (Sedlak, 2010). Cross-cultural comparisons offer similar rates among industrialized nations, with estimates of the prevalence of sexual abuse ranging from 15% to 30% percent of girls and 5% to 15% percent of boys (R. Gilbert et al., 2009). Overall, sexual abuse accounts for 9.5% of cases of substantiated maltreatment in the United States, although this is believed to be an underestimate of its true prevalence: Surveys of adults indicate that a much larger proportion, especially of women, experienced childhood sexual abuse but either did not report it or did not have that report followed up by authorities (see Kerig, Ludlow, & Wenar, 2012).

Although a number of the well-designed longitudinal studies to date include only sexually abused youth in their samples, a few comparative studies suggest that childhood sexual abuse has uniquely pernicious effects on adolescent development (Fergusson, Boden, & Horwood, 2008; Fergusson, McLeod, & Horwood, 2013; Trickett, Negriff, et al., 2011; Walsh, Galea, & Koenen, 2012), particularly in regard to the emergence of aggression and delinquent behavior (P. Cohen, Smailes, & Brown, 2004; Grasso et al., 2013; Herrera & McCloskey, 2003). In addition, childhood sexual abuse is a powerful predictor of adolescent suicidal ideation, suicide attempts, and self-harming behavior (Brodsky et al., 2008) as well as of risky sexual behavior such as unprotected intercourse; for example, sexual abuse is associated with a twofold increase in teenage pregnancy among girls (Noll, Trickett, & Putnam, 2003).

Male Family Members are the Most Typical Perpetrators of Sexual Abuse

Turning to the question of who would sexually abuse a teenager, the research suggests that the risk of perpetration by male family members observed in school-age children continues in adolescence. Overwhelmingly, the perpetrators of adolescents are male relatives; however, there is no one psychological profile that describes the sex offender population (M. Chaffin, Letourneau, & Silovsky, 2002). Moreover, the onset of dating in adolescence brings with it a new source of risk, and that is intimate partner violence. Girls with histories of childhood maltreatment, particularly sexual abuse, are highly vulnerable to choosing antisocial dating partners who revictimize them (Haynie, Giordano, Manning, & Longmore, 2005; Oudekerk & Reppucci, 2009). Furthermore, girls maltreated at home are disproportionately likely to date partners who are significantly older—in some studies, by an average of more than 6 years (Odgers, Moretti, & Reppucci, 2010)—and so their maltreatment by these male adults qualifies as yet another form of child abuse.

PSYCHOLOGICAL ABUSE

As with earlier developmental periods, adolescents who have experienced childhood psychological abuse are vulnerable to the development of a range of internalizing problems, including depression, learned helplessness, and low self-esteem, as well as difficulties related to emotion regulation, including substance abuse and disordered eating. Psychologically abused teenage girls also report more frequent hospitalizations, somatic complaints, and a poor overall sense of well-being (Hart et al., 2011). In addition, longitudinal research shows that psychological abuse in the preschool years is associated with increased aggressiveness in adolescence (Herrenkohl, Egolf, & Herrenkohl, 1997). Overall, negative views of both the self and other seem to stem from parental psychological abuse and to interfere with adolescents' ability to get their emotional needs met in healthy ways in subsequent relationships (Kerig et al., 2012).

Some comparative studies have suggested that psychological maltreatment has more pernicious effects on adolescent mental health than do neglect, sexual abuse, physical abuse, or exposure to domestic violence and, in fact, the co-occurrence of psychological maltreatment appears to exacerbate the effects of other forms of abuse (R. A. McGee, Wolfe, & Wilson, 1997). "The expression of anger, coldness, or hatred that accompanies the physical act of parental aggression could well be more detrimental than the act itself" (Chang, Schwartz, Dodge, & McBride-Chang, 2003, p. 603).

PHYSICAL ABUSE

As we noted earlier, whereas adolescents account for only about 20% of substantiated child abuse reports in the United States, the forms of parent-to-child physical aggression that result in children being identified as physically abused tend to be severe. Furthermore, although the prevalence of physical abuse is higher for boys when they are young, girls are most likely to be abused between the ages of 12 and 15, and therefore adolescence is a time of increased risk for girls (U.S. Department of Health and Human Services, Administration for Children and Families, 2010). In addition, one comparative study suggests that childhood physical abuse has a stronger relationship to adolescent externalizing behavior than do other forms of maltreatment (Herrenkohl et al., 1997).

IMPLICATIONS FOR DEVELOPMENT

Peer Relationships Take Center Stage in Adolescence

Maltreatment in all its forms is associated with compromised peer relationships in adolescence, including an increased risk for both perpetration against and victimization by others (Kerig & Becker, 2015; Trickett, Negriff, et al., 2011). It is not difficult to see why this might be so. As we have seen, histories of neglect and abuse "disrupt the development of capacities the that undergird the formation of healthy and mutually satisfying close personal relationships in adolescence . . . including trust, mutuality of autonomy, relational security, affect regulation, and adaptive interpersonal problem-solving strategies" (Kerig, 2014b, p. 9).

Another reason why the interpersonal effects of maltreatment might become especially salient in adolescence is that the stage-salient demands of the period particularly emphasize relational capacities and thus reveal underlying deficits in these skills. Peer relationships become extremely important sources of self-esteem, belonging, and support in adolescence, and the teenager who is unable to confidently forge such bonds may feel their absence deeply. Moreover, the increasing depth and complexity of adolescent relationships may challenge youths' interpersonal capacities in new ways. This is particularly likely to be the case for romantic relationships, and a strong body of research confirms that all types of childhood maltreatment are associated with disruptions in intimate attachments (see Trickett, Negriff, et al., 2011). Clinical observations also suggest that the emergence of sexuality in adolescence might reveal "sleeper effects" (Beitchman, Zucker, Hood, & DaCosta, 1992)—that is, children who previously appeared to be coping adaptively with childhood maltreatment may become symptomatic in adolescence when they are triggered by the onset of sexual feelings or expectations that they engage in sexual intimacy for which they are not prepared (S. A. McGee & Holmes, 2011).

Other interpersonal consequences for youth who have been the victims of sexual abuse include higher levels of risky sexual activity, coercive sexual behavior, and unhealthy attitudes toward sexuality (Negriff, Noll, Shenk, Putnam, & Trickett, 2010). Particular risks for girls include teenage pregnancy as well as fear of intimacy and dissatisfaction with their romantic relationships. Their dissatisfaction with those relationships may be well founded: Strikingly, studies have found that as many as 45% of sexually abused girls experienced violence at the hands of a dating partner (Cyr, McDuff, & Wright, 2006). The phenomenon of revictimization is not well understood, but a number of theories have been offered, including that experiencing interpersonal violence early in life interferes with adolescents' capacity to recognize and adaptively respond to threats to safety in subsequent intimate relationships (Orcutt, Erickson, & Wolfe, 2002).

However, other research indicates that childhood maltreatment is predictive of aggression against dating partners by both boys and girls (Ehrensaft et al., 2003; Feiring, Simon, Cleland, & Barrett, 2013).

On the positive side, friendship quality can act as protective factor for maltreated adolescents. As Salzinger, Rosario, and Feldman (2007) found in their 6-year follow-up of a sample of children with substantiated physical abuse, lower levels of delinquency among adolescents' circle of friends significantly decreased the risk of delinquency, whereas abuse at the hands of best friends exacerbated the risk.

Adolescence Brings New and More Serious Ways to Get Into Trouble

Closely related to the negative consequences of abuse and neglect on their interpersonal development, adolescents who were maltreated as children also tend to gravitate toward antisocial peer groups, perhaps because it is there that they feel a greater sense of acceptance or belonging. Consorting with antisocial peers in turn is a powerful predictor of engagement in delinquency, substance use, risky sex, and other forms of problem adolescent behavior (Trickett, Negriff, et al., 2011), and some research suggests that these effects are even more pronounced for girls (Widom & White, 1997), particularly because their deviant peer group often includes in a starring role an older, antisocial boyfriend who encourages problem behavior (Kerig, 2014a).

Moreover, childhood abuse is a potent predictor of the more serious forms of delinquent behavior that involve adolescents in the juvenile justice system. Prospective studies find that those abused or neglected as children have 55% higher rates of arrest for nonviolent crimes in late adolescence compared with those who were not maltreated and that the risk of violent crime is increased 96%; moreover, maltreated children begin their criminal careers at younger ages than their peers and are more likely to become chronic offenders (Widom, 2003). Other studies find that those who were abused or neglected in childhood are 4.8 times more likely to be arrested as juveniles, 2 times more likely to be arrested in adulthood, and 11 times more likely to commit a violent crime compared with those not maltreated in childhood (English, Widom, & Brandford, 2002). The association between maltreatment and delinquency emerges in studies of all-girl samples, as well. Childhood physical and sexual abuse are associated with an increased severity of girls' delinquency over the course of 7 years (Cernkovich, Lanctôt, & Giordano, 2008), and sexual abuse predicts girls' risk for later antisocial behavior into adolescence (Trickett & Gordis, 2004) and even adulthood (Trickett, Noll, & Putnam, 2011).

There also are reasons to view parental maltreatment as directly causal to adolescents' involvement in the juvenile justice system. Youth attempting to escape from a maltreating home may run away and resort to "survival crimes," such as theft, prostitution, and drug dealing, in an attempt to subsist on the streets (Chesney-Lind & Pasko, 2004; Kaufman & Widom, 1999; Kerig & Becker, 2012). Street life in turn exposes youth to the risk of being revictimized (Kim, Cicchetti, Rogosch, & Manly, 2009). Even more concerning is that rejecting and maltreating parents may be directly responsible for their adolescents' incarceration: Researchers examining the actual arrest reports of incarcerated girls report many "mutually combative exchanges" in the home that end with parents pressing charges against their "incorrigible" teenagers (Acoca, 1999; Chesney-Lind & Belknap, 2004).

Disruptions in Emotion Regulation Persist for Maltreated Adolescents

As with all other developmental periods, disruption in the capacity to regulate emotions is believed to comprise one of the key mechanisms through which childhood neglect and abuse results in adolescent behavioral and emotional problems (Burnette, Oshri, Lax, Richards, & Ragbeer, 2012; Cicchetti & Toth, 2005; Ford & Courtois, 2009). Moreover, although often viewed as a form of delinquent behavior, one maladaptive method through which maltreated adolescents might attempt to regulate emotions is through substance abuse (Grella & Joshi, 2003). This has emerged as a particularly strong risk factor for maltreated girls who, compared with boys, are both more vulnerable to developing substance abuse problems (Lansford, Dodge, Pettit, & Bates, 2010) and more likely to report using drugs or alcohol as means to cope with upsetting feelings rather than for recreation (Ballon, Courbasson, & Smith, 2001). Furthermore, substance abuse mediates the association between childhood maltreatment and later antisocial behavior for girls, but not for boys (Widom, Schuck, & White, 2006). Research on posttraumatic stress reactions among maltreated adolescents also points toward disrupted emotion regulation in the form of emotional numbing (difficulty identifying or experiencing feelings) and dysphoric arousal (irritability, poor sleep, and difficulty concentrating; Bennett, Kerig, Chaplo, McGee, & Baucom, 2014).

For some adolescents, a disruption in emotion regulation may be related to dissociation (Putnam, 1997). Being unable to identify feelings, self-harm and suicidal behaviors, and aggression have all been linked to dissociative experiences in adolescents (Armstrong, Putnam, Carlson, Libero, & Smith, 1997; Chaplo, Kerig, Bennett, & Modrowski, 2015; Noll, Trickett, & Putnam, 2003; Swannell et al., 2012).

School Disengagement Can Turn to School Failure

The negative effects of abuse on cognitive skills, academic performance, and achievement motivation that we have seen in earlier periods continue into adolescence and are particularly pronounced among those who have experienced neglect (L. A. Sroufe et al., 2005; Veltman & Browne, 2001). Attempts to better understand the psychological mechanisms linking childhood maltreatment to adolescent maladaptation also have focused on cognitive factors, including the meaning that these youth make of their experiences. For example, antisocial attitudes such as alienation from others (Egeland, Yates, Appleyard, & van Dulmen, 2002) and approval of deviant behavior (Brezina, 1998) have been found to mediate the association between child abuse and adolescent delinquency. Focusing on a sample of sexually abused girls, Feiring and colleagues (Feiring, Miller-Johnson, & Cleland, 2007; Feiring et al., 2013; Feiring, Taska, & Lewis, 2002; Simon, Feiring, & McElroy, 2010) have found self-attributions such as shame and stigma to play an important role, with sexually abused girls who report higher levels of shame also having poor-quality friendships and low peer acceptance. In addition, in their longitudinal research, posttraumatic shame and stigma have been shown to be associated with subsequent increasing anger, involvement with antisocial peers, and delinquency. In turn, parental rejection in the context of maltreatment is associated with proneness to shame and depression in adolescence (Stuewig & McCloskey, 2005).

IMPLICATIONS FOR PREVENTION AND INTERVENTION

Posttraumatic Stress Interventions

As with the younger age groups, the most well-validated intervention for trauma among maltreated adolescents is trauma-focused cognitive behavioral therapy (J. A. Cohen, Mannarino, & Deblinger, 2006). As with young children, challenges to implementing the treatment with the adolescent population arise when the parent is the source of the child's trauma. Cognitive processing therapy is a well-established alternative that has been adapted for use with sexually abused teenagers and becomes particularly appropriate with increasing cognitive sophistication and the ability to engage in meta-cognition—that is, "thinking about thinking" in adolescence (Chard, 2005; Matulis, Resick, Rosner, & Steil, 2013).

As we have noted, a particular risk outcome for maltreated adolescents is engaging in misbehaviors that get them into trouble with the juvenile justice system (Kerig & Becker, 2010). Recognition of the significant proportion of juvenile justice–involved youth who have experienced trauma, including parental neglect and maltreatment, has inspired the development of a number of promising programs designed with this specific population in mind. Premiere among these is *Trauma Affect Regulation: Guide for Education and Therapy* (TARGET), an empirically supported intervention that combines individual, group, and milieu treatment to enhance youths' capacities for affect regulation in the aftermath of complex trauma (J. D. Ford & Blaustein, 2013; Ford & Hawke, 2012; Ford, Steinberg, Hawke, Levine, & Zhang, 2012; Marrow, Knudsen, Olafson, & Bucher, 2013). A number of other promising treatments that are being developed for traumatized adolescents in detention and residential settings are described in a special issue of the *Journal of Family Violence* (Pond & Spinazzola, 2013).

Dating Violence Prevention Programs for Maltreated Teens

Although "universal" dating violence prevention programs such as Safe Dates (Foshee & Langwick, 2004) may reach maltreated teens in the schools where they are implemented, other "targeted" programs have been designed specifically for those who are at risk because of a history of maltreatment in the home (Wolfe et al., 1997). Expect Respect (Rosenbluth, 2004) is one such intervention that has been demonstrated to be effective in reducing at-risk teens' acceptance and perpetration of aggression against intimate partners (Ball, Kerig, & Rosenbluth, 2009). Boys and girls meet in separate support groups led by trained staff who use a 24-week curriculum to guide sessions focused on five core units: communication skills and group cohesion, choosing equality and respect, recognizing abusive relationships, learning skills for establishing and maintaining healthy relationships, and getting the message out. A unique part of the intervention is a concluding session in which girls' and boys' groups convene together to ask "everything you ever wanted to know but we afraid to ask" questions of one another and to share the lessons they have learned about positive relationships.

Mentoring

Mentoring is a popular intervention strategy for adolescents in general, and youth aging out of foster care in particular (Ahrens, DuBois, Richardson, Fan, & Lozano, 2008; DuBois, Portillo, Rhodes, Silverthorn, & Valentine, 2011). It strikes many that these youth lack positive role models and that introducing some at the time when youth are making crucial decisions makes intuitive sense. The data show a more complicated picture. Mentoring does work, when mentors and youth form an enduring relationship (Grossman & Rhodes, 2002; Rhodes, Haight, & Briggs, 1999). Forming a relationship is not easy for youth who have a history of betrayal, abuse, and neglect in their relationships with their closest caregivers. When youth do not embrace the relationship, there can be a tendency to blame them for not taking advantage of the help that is offered. For mentors who are accustomed to caring, reciprocal relationships and who believe in the power of mentoring, it can be confusing and hurtful to be rejected. Some successful programs target youth who show signs of being likely to succeed in a mentoring relationship (Schwartz, Rhodes, Chan, & Herrera, 2011). More research is needed to make definitive recommendations for mentors who are working with youth who are likely to have difficulty forming relationships. For now, professionals can consider the role of attachment style (Larose, Bernier, & Tarabulsy, 2005). Mentors may benefit from education about attachment styles, and youth may benefit from different approaches if they have avoidant or ambivalent attachment styles.

POSTTRAUMATIC STRESS AND DISSOCIATION

As children mature into adolescence, posttraumatic and dissociative processes manifest in new ways. As time goes on, it becomes more difficult to disentangle the effects of maltreatment from other traumatic and stressful life events that co-occur. However, there is some evidence that preschool maltreatment continues to be associated with posttraumatic stress and dissociation symptoms in adolescents. Lansford et al. (2002) measured physical abuse in children the summer before they began kindergarten and again when they reached 11th grade. Those children who were physically abused before kindergarten had more posttraumatic stress disorder (PTSD) and dissociation symptoms at the 11th-grade time point. This was true even after the researchers controlled for many other factors, including exposure to violence and harsh parental treatment during adolescence.

In adolescence, dissociation is related to a variety of psychiatric problems, including risk taking, suicidality, self-harm, and sexual aggression (Kisiel & Lyons, 2001). PTSD and dissociation also mediate the link between child abuse and revictimization in adolescence (Gobin & Freyd, 2009; Noll et al., 2003).

Clinicians with an interest in dissociation in adolescents have several resources available. Case examples illustrating various dissociative features are found in *Dissociation in Children and Adolescents* (Putnam, 1997), *The Dissociative Child* (Silberg, 1998), and *The Child Survivor* (Silberg, 2013). A measure of dissociation specific to adolescents, the Adolescent Dissociative

Experiences Scale (Armstrong et al., 1997), can be found as an appendix to *Dissociation in Children and Adolescents* (Putnam, 1997).

COMMON MISCONCEPTIONS

Misconception: Adolescents Are at Low Risk for Neglect Because of Their Relative Maturity

Just because adolescents can physically run away from home does not mean that they do or that it makes sense to do so. For a variety of reasons, many adolescents remain in neglectful homes.

Misconception: Boys Are More Likely to be Physically Abused Because They Are More Likely to Have Challenging Behaviors

Another misperception is that adolescent boys are more vulnerable to certain forms of abuse because they engage in more challenging behaviors; however, with the exception of sexual abuse, which is 3 times more likely to occur among girls than boys, there are typically no gender differences found in the rates of neglect and maltreatment (Trickett, Negriff, et al., 2011). An exception to this is the subset of delinquent adolescents who are involved in the juvenile justice system, but in this case, the well-replicated finding is that it is girls, rather than boys, who are more likely to have been the direct victims of violence in the home (Cauffman, 2008; Kerig & Becker, 2012; Kerig, Vanderzee, Becker, & Ward, 2013).

RECOMMENDED RESOURCES

Less Technical

Eriksen, S.-E., Haig, D., Johnson, G., Terhock, L. [Producers], & Scully, L. [Director]. (1996). *Good things too.* Canada: National Film Board of Canada.
   This film is a drama about five teens struggling to survive sexual abuse. As their stories unfold, their past is illuminated by animated flashback sequences. This film shows painful and difficult memories as well as moments of triumph and success.

Littig, E. [Producer & Director], & Long, L. [Producer]. (1990). *A little problem at home*. United States: NEWIST/CESA.
In this video, adult and adolescent children of alcoholics describe their experiences growing up in the home of an alcoholic parent who was also abusive, psychologically or physically.

Pelzer, D. (1997). *The lost boy: A foster child's search for the love of a family*. Deerfield Beach, FL: Health Communications.

Siegel, D. J. (2014). *Brainstorm: The power and purpose of the teenage brain*. New York, NY: Penguin.

Silverman, S. (1996). *Because I remember terror, father, I remember you*. Athens: University of Georgia Press.

More Technical

Blaustein, M. E., & Kinniburgh, K. M. (2010). *Treating traumatic stress in children and adolescents: How to foster resilience through attachment, self-regulation, and competency*. New York, NY: Guilford Press.

Cohen, J. A., Mannarino, A. P., & Deblinger, E. (2012). *Trauma-focused CBT for children and adolescents: Treatment applications*. New York, NY: Guilford Press.

6

Emerging Adulthood

Emerging adulthood is a time for exploration. Today, young people take longer to reach traditional milestones of adulthood than did young people in the past. Emerging adults, generally defined as ages 18 to 25, delay marriage, childbearing, and settling into a home and career later than ever before. Overall, emerging adults report feeling "in between" adolescence and adulthood (Arnett, 2000, 2006, 2014; Settersten & Ray, 2010). Therefore, the phase of emerging adulthood is considered to be an important one under the umbrella of the developmental psychopathology framework, and research shows that the long shadow of maltreatment extends into the stage of the adolescent-to-adult transition (Kerig, Ludlow, & Wenar, 2012). Although some worry that emerging adults will never grow up, the data indicate that by age 30, most young adults have met the traditional milestones associated with adulthood, taking responsibility for themselves, making decisions independently, and becoming financially independent

http://dx.doi.org/10.1037/14898-006
Child Maltreatment: A Developmental Psychopathology Approach, by K. Becker-Blease and P. K. Kerig
Copyright © 2016 by the American Psychological Association. All rights reserved.

(Arnett, 2000). The feeling of being "in between" also slowly dissolves into a feeling of a being an adult (see Figure 6.1).

Jeffrey Jensen Arnett (Arnett, 2000, 2006, 2014) has described five features of the period of emerging adulthood. First, it is an age of identity exploration. Young people generally are freer than in the past to pursue hobbies, careers, courses of study, and so forth to further identify who they are and what they want to do in life. Second, it is an age of instability, characterized by frequent moves between jobs and residences. Third, it is a self-focused age. Most young people want eventually to take on the responsibility of being a partner and parent, but only after spending time developing their own interests. Fourth, it is an age of feeling in between. Emerging adulthood is not just an extended adolescence but a qualitatively different stage of life, distinct from adolescence and adulthood. Fifth, it is an age of possibilities. Emerging adults are extremely optimistic about their ability to pursue their dreams.

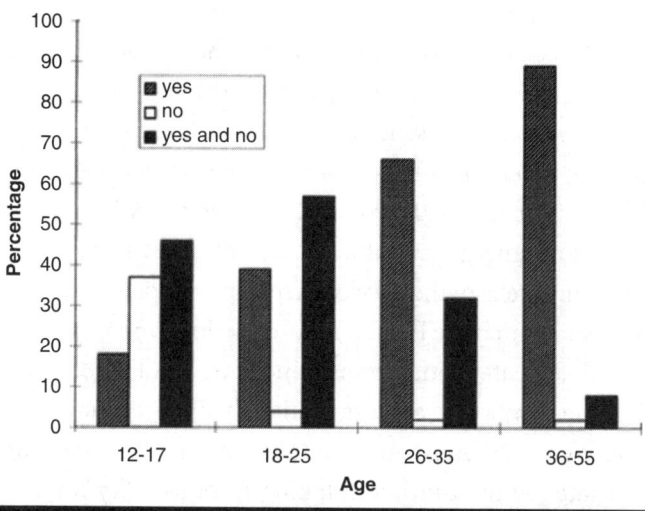

Figure 6.1

Do you feel that you have reached adulthood? $N = 519$. Data are from Arnett (2001). From "Emerging Adulthood: A Theory of Development From the Late Teens Through the Twenties," by J. J. Arnett, 2000, *American Psychologist, 55*, p. 472. Copyright 2000 by the American Psychological Association.

To understand how the stage of emerging adulthood applies to youth leaving homes characterized by maltreatment, it is crucial to understand the historical and social conditions that have given rise to this new developmental stage in modern society. In the previous chapter, we looked at adolescence as a period of risk and resilience, and in some ways emerging adulthood is a continuation of those processes. Young people entering the workplace in the second decade of the 21st century have found few jobs for those with low or even moderate skills, leading them to pursue more education after high school than ever before (Arnett, 2000; C. Ryan & Siebens, 2012). At the same time, parents of emerging adults have, in general, more time and resources to spend on their children than ever before. Emerging adulthood does extend the period of risk, and emerging adults engage in relatively high rates of risk-taking behavior, including drug use (Arnett, 2005). For the most part, spending additional time defining an identity and developing skills with the financial and emotional support of parents is beneficial.

The question is, do the typical observed benefits of emerging adulthood also flow to youth emerging from riskier homes? On the one hand, maltreated youth could benefit from an extended period of exploration and identity formation. In particular, in the past, foster parents raced to get foster youth ready for complete independence by age 18. If this is no longer expected socially, foster youth may benefit from some extended time and support while they explore issues of identity, work, and relationships. For example, youth who struggle with interpersonal relationships may in the past have been pushed into marriages before they were ready, whereas today, those youth may learn interpersonal skills through their 20s that translate into more successful marriages.

On the other hand, if this period of growth depends on committed parents' financial and emotional support, then maltreated youth without such resources could be at additional disadvantage. Also, if the period of emerging adulthood is characterized by a longer period of risk-taking behavior, at-risk youth could be especially vulnerable to drug addiction and other poor outcomes. This leads to important questions for foster care practice and policy and also for the larger question of how to support youth who emerge from maltreating homes directly. Some research has begun in this area (Becker-Blease, Tucker, & Holt, 2008; Masten, Obradović, & Burt, 2006), and much more is needed.

FOR FOSTER YOUTH, THE TRANSITION TO INDEPENDENCE IS CHANGING

In the United States, the Foster Care Independence Act (1999) provides federal money for states to administer programs designed to assist youth transitioning from foster care to independent living. The typical focus of these programs is practical life skills, such as budgeting, obtaining a job, setting up a household, and other activities of daily living. Transitioning youth work with their caseworkers and independent living staff to create independent living plans, based on individual youth's goals for the future. In recent years, some provisions have been made for youth after age 18. In some states, youth can remain in foster care until age 21. In others, Medicaid has been made available to former foster youth until age 21.

Youth typically take the Ansell-Casey Life Skills Assessment (Casey Family Programs, n.d.) to determine skill levels. Youth then work with independent living program staff to choose the skills most relevant to them and to develop a plan to meet their goals. The process is designed to be youth centered, both in providing information on which skills are necessary for a successful transition to independent living and for allowing youth considerable input into which skills to focus on and how to learn those skills.

Just how successful independent living programs are is unclear (Lemon, Hines, & Merdinger, 2005). Whereas independent living programs are mandated to provide and evaluate the effectiveness of their services, even when programs are youth focused, it is often quite difficult to engage older adolescents and emerging adults in programs and evaluation studies. Programs vary considerably from location to location and year to year. Because emerging adults are more dependent than ever on parents, the gap between what former foster youth must do for themselves and what typical peers do for themselves is widening. That widening gap makes it difficult to evaluate objectively the accomplishments of former foster youth compared with other youth.

Increasingly, there are calls for reforms in services offered to emerging adults as they leave foster care (Avery & Freundlich, 2009). Those calling for change have made three major points:

1. Because the average family now provides more support to youth through age 25, states should provide more support to former foster youth past the age of 18 or 21.
2. Because there is no substitute for committed older adults in the lives of emerging adults, more should be done to ensure even older youth leave foster care with a permanent family.
3. While skills are necessary for independent living, the focus of programs for emerging adults should shift to include a strong focus on interpersonal relationships. Toward this end, Avery and Freundlich (2009) suggested replacing the phrase *independent living* with *interdependent living*.

THE TRANSITION TO COLLEGE IS DIFFICULT FOR MALTREATED YOUTH

Maltreated youth emerge from a variety of settings: foster homes, residential facilities, group homes, extended family's homes, and biological parents' homes. The challenges maltreated youth face at college are equally varied.

Maltreated youth are less likely than nonmaltreated peers to start and to graduate from college (Blome, 1997; Duncan, 2000). Just why this is so is not well understood. The lack of financial, social, and parental support (Lemon et al., 2005), as well as mental health and academic preparation (Lansford et al., 2002), are major concerns. Sandberg and Lynn (1992) found that college students who reported a history of more psychological and physical abuse also reported more dissociation. Those with high dissociation scores reported lower college adjustment in academic, social, and personal-emotional adjustment and institutional attachment.

Former foster and maltreated youth who are admitted to college lack financial and practical resources necessary for independent living. Students frequently rely on parents for a place to stay during school breaks and funds to cover housing deposits, car repairs, and other nonroutine expenses that financial aid may not cover for even the most frugal students. Independent living programs, nonprofit organizations, and colleges provide some supports to overcome these barriers.

Notably, with few exceptions for youth who have previously spent extensive time in foster care, none of these supports exist for maltreated youth who are not exiting the foster care system. Youth who enroll in college while still living in a home with parents who have been abusive or neglectful, or who leave home to begin college, are essentially invisible. Many colleges do provide a range of supports, such as academic support, food boxes, short-term loans, for example, for students who need it. The extent to which youth from maltreating homes use or benefit from these services is unknown.

SEXUAL ABUSE SURVIVORS STRUGGLE WITH SEXUAL INTIMACY IN DIFFERENT WAYS

Establishing intimate relationships is a significant stage-salient task of emerging adulthood (Montgomery, 2005). Many people who experienced child sexual abuse have some difficulty with sexuality and intimacy as adults (Neumann, Houskamp, Pollock, & Briere, 1996). Davis and Petretic-Jackson (2000) described three patterns of problematic interactions. First, some people who have experienced sexual abuse are able to engage in sexual relationships, but the relationships tend to lack emotional intimacy. The pattern is one of multiple shallow relationships that do not last. A second group of maltreatment survivors fear both sexuality and intimacy and avoid relationships altogether. Third, some survivors fear both sexuality and intimacy but have an overriding desire to be in a relationship with someone. Not knowing who to trust or having difficulty maintaining their identity while in a relationship, these people tend to partner with people who abuse them, and a cycle of violence is perpetuated.

Zurbriggen and Freyd (2004) described several cognitive mechanisms that may be related to problematic sexuality and intimacy. People who used dissociation to cope with sexual abuse as a child may learn to dissociate during sex later in life, making it difficult to clearly interpret information and make sexual decisions. Sandberg, Lynn, and Matorin (2001) found that college women with high dissociations scores rated a video depicting events leading up to acquaintance rape as being less risky than college women with similar levels of other mental health symptoms or with low dissociations scores. Women high in dissociation also identified fewer danger cues when they were asked to list "significant or meaningful events" than the other groups. Interestingly, when the same women were explicitly told the events ended in a sexual assault, there were no differences in groups, suggesting that they had encoded the information but did not bring it to mind and process it in the same way as those with lower dissociation scores. The implication for clinicians and violence prevention trainers is that women, including those who have been previously victimized, may be consciously aware of warning signs and may benefit from programs that help them understand how posttraumatic stress and prior trauma affect sexual victimization specifically.

As evidenced by research, basic risk-detecting mechanisms are likely underdeveloped or damaged in those have been harmed by trusted others, resulting in difficulty choosing safe partners (Delker & Freyd, 2014; Freyd, 1996; Gidycz, McNamara, & Edwards, 2006; Noll & Grych, 2011). Reality testing is likely to be affected as the result of the ways perpetrators and others distort reality with messages such as, "You wanted it." More generally, there may be a set of thoughts and beliefs about the self, access to information about internal states, and decision-making processes that can be thought of as consensual sex decision-making mechanisms that lead to difficulty with sexuality, including avoidance of sexuality and risky sex behaviors (Zurbriggen & Freyd, 2004).

More research is needed on areas of strength and resilience in interpersonal relationships, as well as research that focuses on the couple or family unit as a whole. In one interesting example, Millwood (2011) assessed empathic understanding in couples in which one female partner had a history of child sexual abuse. In this sample, child sexual abuse survivors were less able to correctly identify their partners' thoughts and feelings, but their partners were more capable than were people who were partnered with someone who did not have a history of abuse. One possible explanation is partners of child abuse survivors can compensate for their partner's lack of empathic understanding by going out of their way to better understand the abused partner.

Assessing problems, as well as areas of strength, with sexuality and intimacy is a challenge. Clinicians may find the Trauma Symptom Inventory—2 (Briere, 2010) to be useful. It contains a Sexual Concerns scale as well as an Insecure Attachment scale that might help clinicians both identify and distinguish between problems with sexuality and problems with intimacy more generally. Wendy Maltz, a sex therapist, has published a comparison of characteristics of healthy and unhealthy sex and a checklist of positive aspects of sex at http://www.healthysex.com that may help identify areas of strength or help survivors recognize signs of risk.

MALTREATMENT LEADS TO UNIQUE SUBSTANCE ABUSE CHALLENGES

Given the high prevalence of both maltreatment and substance abuse among emerging adults, clinicians are likely to encounter many clients— particularly women—who report both (Delker & Freyd, 2014; Widom, Schuck, & White, 2006). Furthermore, in line with a model of self-medication, many clients may well state that they use substances to cope with traumatic experiences, including maltreatment. We know that the picture is more complex than this. At a minimum, we know that maltreatment is correlated with a host of other predictors of substance abuse including having parents who model substance abuse and other types of trauma and adversity (e.g., death or incarceration of a parent). It is difficult to know how potent maltreatment is compared with these other covariates. Also, it is likely that a genetic predisposition to addiction, or perhaps to internalizing or externalizing symptoms more generally (Keyes et al., 2012), interacts with the maltreatment experience. Emerging evidence also suggests a role for epigenetics. Although more work needs to be done, it seems like that substance use alters the epigenome in ways that alter behavior and can be passed down to the next generation (Keyes et al., 2012).

As a first step, the data are clear: Statistically, maltreatment is related to substance abuse. In a large birth cohort sample, Fergusson, Boden, and Horwood (2008) found that retrospective reports of child physical and sexual abuse were related to substance dependence as measured by a clinical interview. The severity of abuse was positively associated with rates of substance dependence. Emerging adults who had experienced sexual abuse with attempted or completed penetration were especially likely to meet *Diagnostic and Statistical Manual of Mental Disorders* (4th ed.; American Psychiatric Association, 2000) criteria for substance dependence (see Figure 6.2). Fully 20% of people ages 21 to 25, and 25% of those ages 18 to 21 with a history of attempted or completed sexual abuse met criteria for substance abuse.

Physical, sexual, and emotional abuse and physical neglect are related to substance abuse. Goldstein et al. (2013) examined alcohol use and several types of abuse and neglect in a large, representative sample of emerging adults. They found that a history of physical, sexual, and emotional abuse and physical neglect were each independently related to higher rates of alcohol use disorder. However, once controlling for other mental health disorders and other factors, no association remained. This finding suggests

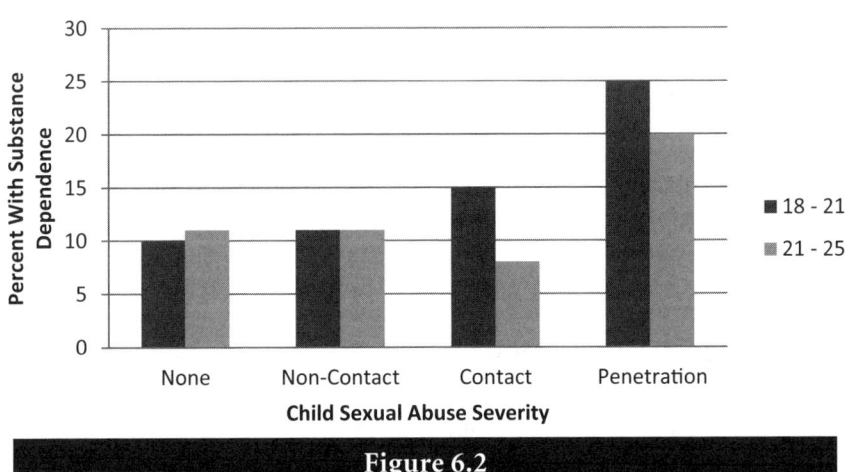

Figure 6.2

The more severe the child sexual abuse, the more likely emerging adults meet criteria for substance dependence. Data from Fergusson, Boden, and Horwood (2008).

that emerging adults with a history of maltreatment are likely to need treatment for both substance abuse and co-occurring mental health symptoms.

Goldstein et al. (2013) went further, asking whether there are differences in barriers to treatment for those who have experienced maltreatment. Interestingly, financial concerns did not seem to differ between those who had or had not experienced maltreatment. However, those who had experienced maltreatment were more likely to endorse reasons that may indicate a distrust of others, including statements such as, "didn't think anyone could help" and "thought I should be strong enough to handle it alone." This finding reinforces the point that a focus on relationships be a key focus of treatment in this population.

IMPLICATIONS FOR PREVENTION AND INTERVENTION

Clinicians and others who work with emerging adults who have experienced maltreatment would do well to make focusing on interpersonal relationships a goal of their work with their clients. Social isolation, relationship difficulty, social anxiety, and negative thoughts about the self and others are both symptoms and consequences of several mental health disorders. Strengthening the client's capacity to engage in safe, supportive relationships as a primary focus of the therapy may not only increase the success of the therapeutic encounter with the clinician but may also allow for the development of an important social support network (Herman, 1997).

We have reasonable evidence to suggest that the transition from foster care is particularly challenging. Even with the support described here, many former foster youth do not fare well in the transition to adulthood. It should give us pause, then, to remember that none of these services exist for youth independently transitioning from maltreating homes. Clinicians working with youth who are leaving maltreating homes without the benefit of the supports provided to youth transitioning from foster care have their work cut out for them. As with foster youth, a focus on interpersonal relationships and building social support may be an early goal of therapy.

Much more work is needed to tease apart the interrelated factors that predict substance abuse in emerging adulthood. We know little, for example, about how genes interact with maltreatment experiences to lead to substance use and abuse or whether children inherit an epigenome that is marked by their parents' substance use. For now, it is clear that those foster parents, clinicians, and others who work with people who have a history of maltreatment should be well versed in substance abuse prevention and treatment. The data suggest that it may be particularly important to help emerging adults with a history of maltreatment to find effective treatment for other mental health disorders and to build trust with treatment providers.

COMMON MISCONCEPTIONS

Misconception: Young People Today "Fail to Launch"

Some people are concerned when young people do not establish their own household and gain financial independence in their early 20s. The evidence suggests that this is not a failure to launch but rather a developmental period of identity development and exploration. Most young people do become independent adults by age 30.

Misconception: Those Who Were Abused Will Abuse Others

A common misperception is that those who grew up in maltreating homes will inevitably become abusive to their own intimate partners or, when they become parents, to their children. The best estimate of the risk of intergenerational transmission is approximately 30% (Egeland et al., 2002), which means that the majority of individuals who were maltreated do in fact manage to break the cycle. Of the protective factors that have been identified, one seems to emerge with particular consistency in the research, and that is when abuse survivors are able to form a relationship with a partner who provides them with empathy, support, and a model of a different kind of intimacy.

RECOMMENDED RESOURCES

Less Technical

Brown, L. S. (2015). *Not the price of admission: Healthy relationships after childhood trauma.* Seattle, WA: CreateSpace.
This evidence-based how-to guide is for anyone who experienced child maltreatment and wants to create healthier relationships with friends and romantic partners.

Casey Life Skills. (n.d.). Retrieved from http://lifeskills.casey.org
This free online assessment and resource guide is aimed at helping youth in foster care, ages 14 to 21, identify and learn skills needed for independent living.

FosterClub. (2006). *Permanency pact.* Retrieved from http://www.fosterclub.com/_transition/article/permanency-pact
This free guide helps a facilitator connect a foster youth with a supportive adult. Potential uses go beyond this. The guide includes a list of 45 ways an adult can support a youth—everything from a place to do laundry to legal help. This list reminds us the gaps that maltreated youth—in foster care or not—often have, and serves as a starting point to help youth find ways to get their needs met.

Maltz, W. (2012). *Sexual healing journey* (3rd ed.). New York, NY: William Morrow Paperbacks.
This self-help book is a practical guide to establishing safe and satisfying sexual relationships, a common challenge for those who have experienced sexual abuse. The companion website (http://www.healthysex.com) has additional free resources.

More Technical

Behavioral Tech website. Retrieved from http://www.behavioraltech.org
Founded by Marsha Linehan, Behavioral Tech provides training and resources to clinicians in dialectical behavior therapy, an especially promising approach for working with adolescents and young adults who harm themselves, are suicidal, or have difficulty with relationships and emotions.

Najavits, L. M. (2002). *Seeking safety: A treatment manual for PTSD and substance abuse.* New York, NY: Guilford Press.
This manual for mental health professionals explains a flexible manualized approach to working with thoughts, behaviors, and relationships as experienced by clients with both posttraumatic stress disorder and substance abuse concerns.

Afterword

This monograph is appearing at a key moment in time for child abuse research and related clinical work. Over the past two decades or so, we have gained important data from medical, public health, developmental, mental health, and criminal perspectives that allow the promise of true progress.

Crime data and surveys indicate that child physical abuse and sexual abuse crimes have declined dramatically, and child neglect has declined as well. As Finkelhor, Jones, Shattuck, and Saito (2013) explained, it is possible that this decline is real and multifactorial:

> The period when sexual and physical abuse started the dramatic downward trend was marked by sustained economic improvement, increases in the numbers of law enforcement and child protection personnel, more aggressive prosecution and incarceration policies, growing public awareness about the problems, and the dissemination of new treatment options for family and mental health problems, including new psychiatric medication. (p. 3)

As a developmental psychopathology perspective would suggest, the improvement is likely the result of transactions among multiple factors acting at many levels, from individual to societal, that cross professional boundaries to include criminal justice, public health, religious, educational, sociological, and psychological effects.

At the same time, a wave of social and legal action has raised awareness of the vulnerability, especially for late-adolescent girls and emerging adult women in and out of college. Developmental psychopathology perspectives are needed to solve this problem. Clearly, young people enter college and emerging adulthood with experiences in families and schools and with peers and dating partners that lead to high risk at a developmentally important transition. Making children safer will ultimately lead to making emerging adults safer. At the same time, some data suggest that women on college campuses are at increased risk compared with noncollege peers (B. S. Fisher, Cullen, & Turner, 2000; Sampson, 2002). Researchers and clinicians alike must better understand the context of abuse and its effects across the lifespan and across contexts.

Researchers and clinicians are now well positioned to undertake the kind of multidisciplinary, developmentally informed work needed to understand not only what might work to prevent abuse and enhance resilience in maltreated children in the future but also what is working in the present. Today, researchers, school administrators, public health officials, and clinicians have access to free, open-source, validated measures of victimization, such as the Juvenile Victimization Questionnaire (Finkelhor, Hamby, Turner, & Ormrod, 2011) and the Administer Researcher Campus Climate Consortium's campus climate survey (available at http://campusclimate.gsu.edu). As discussed in this book, it is also possible to test promising programs with randomized controlled trials to target even more precisely the best prevention and intervention strategies that will be most effective for the most people. It is possible to make truly effective mental health treatment available to children at the time abuse is identified. As churches, K–12 schools, universities, and other organizations work to reduce the risk of abuse within their ranks, it is possible that we will have fewer children who experience the devastating effects of abuse and victimization. These outcomes are achievable—and indeed are happening—and we now have the scientific and clinical expertise within developmental psychopathology to see the job through.

Appendix

APPENDIX

Table 1
Overview of Normative Development

	Infancy/toddlerhood	Preschool age	School age	Early adolescence	Late adolescence/emerging adulthood
Stage-salient issues	Attachment, basic trust, affect regulation, autonomous self	Self-regulation, peer relations, empathy, gender roles	Mastery of academic and social environments	Individuation, identity; sexuality; gender role; social acceptance	Independence from family, formation of intimate relationships
Cognitive development	Understand through sensing and doing, object permanence and object constancy develop	Preoperational magical thinking, egocentric, assimilation of new experiences to existing schemas	Concrete and logical, black-and-white thinking, need to label and organize experience; react to events experienced in mind rather than reality (e.g., fears, fantasies, appraisals)	Metacognition and abstraction emerge, able to consider hypotheses	Formal logic and abstract thought
Language development	Development of language, ability to express wants and needs in more purposeful way	Rapid acquisition of language, cognitively organize and manipulate experience	Increasing vocabulary, ability to present coherent narratives	Expanding and fine-tuning, especially for emotion terms with finer gradations	Further expansion and development

APPENDIX

Memory development	Experiential; not mediated, organized, or labeled by language; triggered readily and with intense affect by reminiscent stimuli	Memories grouped and evoked by events with similar salient affect, experiences conflated	Retrieved according to emotional tone or similarity of experience; events and accompanying feelings recalled as "facts"	Conception of time consistent with reality, retrieve information in temporal order	Memory temporal
Attachment	Caregiver as secure base	Internal working model of self and other	Goal-directed partnership	Reemergence of conflict over proximity vs. independence	Formation of new attachments allows reworking of old ones
Self development	Experiences defined by reference to caregivers (e.g., loved self is lovable) Self-constancy emerges	Behavioral self: defined by "all-or-none" abilities and actions	Psychological self: stable internal representation, difficulty resolving inconsistencies	Self more integrated, complex, self-reflective	Increasingly stable, complex, internalized
Emotional development	Emotions driven by immediate experience; labile, primary, and intense	Language about emotions expands, as do heightened displays of feelings (temper tantrums, fears); view emotions as caused by external events; use pretend play to describe, act out, regulate emotions	Affects more stable, affective "style" emerges, capacity for internally generated emotions	Labile emotions, negative affect common	Stable affect regulation, capacity for full range of emotions and defenses against them

(*continues*)

107

APPENDIX

Table 1
Overview of Normative Development (*Continued*)

	Infancy/toddlerhood	Preschool age	School age	Early adolescence	Late adolescence/emerging adulthood
Moral development	Limited	Preconventional: simplistic, literal, absolute	Conventional: rule-bound, right vs. wrong, internalize parents' rules into conscience, guilt	Considerations of mutuality, perspective taking	Can generate own moral principles
Social development	Focused on relations with caregivers, egocentric	Increasing peer interactions, social comparison, increasing recognition of others' emotions	Friendships and relations with teachers important, social perspective taking, gender differences intensify	Group-oriented relationships with peers increasingly important, social problem solving	Romantic relationships Peers have increasing importance over family
Family development	Infant is entirely dependent on parents to define meaning of events and provide safety and comfort	Parents must tolerate vacillation between dependency and independent strivings	Family's functioning is viewed in increasingly public realms, which can impart shame or acclaim	Family boundaries must become more flexible and shift to allow adolescent's independence	Realignment of relationships to allow adolescent to function as young adult

Note. Data from Cicchetti and Toth (1998); Cohen, Mannarino, and Deblinger (2012); Kerig, Ludlow, and Wenar (2012); Kruczek and Vitanza (2015); Phillips and Shonkoff (2000); Pynoos (1993); Sameroff and Fiese (2000); and Sroufe (1986).

APPENDIX

Table 2
Developmental Processes Disrupted by Exposure to Maltreatment and Violence

	Infancy/toddlerhood	Preschool age	School age	Early adolescence	Late adolescence/emerging adulthood
Stage-salient issues	Basic mistrust, anxiety about ability to get emotional needs met	Self-regulation and autonomy disrupted: leading to excessive control of self (internalizing) or environment (externalizing)	Perceived incompetence in academic and social environments	Premature or delayed individuation from family, rigid or negative perceptions of gender roles	Transmission of violence into own intimate relationships
Cognitive development	Insecurity inhibits exploration of environment and new learning. Developmental delays	Vulnerable to cognitive confusions, distorted appraisals that interfere with reasoning about violence	Poor concentration and low school achievement. Negative cognitions and distorted appraisals; perceived control and responsibility regarding violence	School failure or dropout, foreclosure of opportunities for intellectual development	School failure or drop out, foreclosure of opportunities for intellectual development. Risky decision making
Attachment development	Insecure attachment	Insecure and negative internal working models of self and other	Insecure and negative schema replicated in relations with peers and teachers	Distrust in self and others leads to risky and self-harming behavior	Interpersonal distrust, unrealistically positive or negative expectations of relationships

(*continues*)

109

APPENDIX

Table 2
Developmental Processes Disrupted by Exposure to Maltreatment and Violence (*Continued*)

	Infancy/toddlerhood	Preschool age	School age	Early adolescence	Late adolescence/ emerging adulthood
Self development	Negative self-representations	Low self-esteem	Stable negative internal representation of self Depression, self-blame (especially girls)	Poor self-esteem, depression, shame Dissociation related to a fragmented self	Poor self-esteem, depression
Emotional development	Unregulated distress Poor emotion regulation skills Difficulty expressing emotions appropriately	Diffuse anger, anxiety Poor emotion regulation Limited emotion lexicon	Anger, hopelessness, anxiety Poor emotion regulation Negative affect consolidates into schema generalized to all new experiences	Diffuse anger, hopelessness, anxiety Disillusionment and moodiness	Restricted range of affect Depression Suicidality and non-suicidal self-injury
Moral development		Identification with aggressor Limited empathy, maladaptive responses to others' distress	Belief that violence is justified and normative Disrespect for females, rigid and stereotypic sex-roles (especially boys)	Belief that violence is justified Disrespect for females, gender-role stereotyping	Disrespect for females, gender-role stereotypes Foreshortened future, "live for the moment"

APPENDIX

Social development	Aggression, withdrawal, poor social skills	Aggression and inability to regulate emotions negatively affect peer relations Sensitization and overreactivity to aggression in others	Withdrawal and/or aggression result in negative peer relations and rejection	Difficulty forming close relationships and managing dependency needs Association with negative peer group	Recapitulations of victim–victimizer roles in romantic relationships Association with negative peer group Less empathy in dating relationships
Family relations	Cope by seeking comfort from caregiver; caregiver's response will determine outcome Attempts to comfort or distract parents may put child at risk	Stress may result in parental harshness or unavailability Aggression toward mother, blaming mother for violence	Oppositionality and attempts to intervene increase risk of spillover onto child (especially boys) Guilt over not preventing violence	Alienation from family or enmeshment Perceived responsibility to provide care or protection to mother (especially girls)	Alienation from family or enmeshment (e.g., child as caregiver or protector to parent)
Memory for trauma	Memories accompanied by disorganized, intense, affects easily triggered by reminiscent stimuli	Traumatic events and related affects conflated and distorted	Events and accompanying feelings recalled as "facts" Able to experience complex and ambivalent emotions	Numbing, denial, avoidance of trauma-related cues	Numbing, denial, avoidance of trauma-related cues

Note. Data from Cicchetti and Toth (1995); Connolly (2014); Kerig (2003); Kerig, Ludlow, and Wenar (2012); Lieberman and Knorr (2007); Millwood (2011); Moffitt (2013); Nock (2010); Ogawa, Sroufe, Weinfield, Carlson, and Egeland (1997); Putnam (1997); Pynoos (1993); Silberg (2013); and Weller, Leve, Kim, Bhimji, and Fisher (2015).

APPENDIX

Table 3
Developmental Impact of Exposure to Maltreatment and Violence and Considerations for Intervention

	Infancy/toddlerhood	Preschool age	School age	Early adolescence	Late adolescence/ emerging adulthood
Stage-salient issues	Secure attachment, balance dependence and independence	Self-regulation, autonomy, gender identify	Mastery of academic and social realms	Identity, finding one's place	Individuation from family
Risk outcomes	Unregulated distress Failure to thrive Disruption in eating/sleeping Developmental delays Insecure/disorganized attachment PTSD	Externalizing, peer aggression Insecure attachment, clinginess, anxiety Sensitization to inter-adult aggression Boys more internalizing, externalizing, somatic symptoms PTSD	Increasing behavior problems Aggression, oppositionality, bullying, poor peer relations Disrespect for females; gender-role stereotypes Depression, low self-esteem Anxiety, withdrawal Low school achievement, poor concentration PTSD	Dating violence, bullying Truancy, runaway, negative peer group Disrespect for females, gender-role stereotypes Poor self-esteem, depression (especially girls), suicide Avoidant coping style Decline in school achievement PTSD and dissociation	High school and college dropout Early parenthood Substance abuse Internalizing and externalizing problems Psychosis

112

APPENDIX

PTSD symptoms	Repetitive, reenactment play, which may or may not be overtly distressing; distress at reminders; numbing response (constriction of play, socially withdrawn, restricted range of affect) Regression Night terrors, nightmares, sleep difficulty, fear of the dark Aggression, separation anxiety, fears	Repetitive play, nightmares, night terrors, intrusive images, trauma reenactment, separation/stranger anxiety, regression, eating problems, sensitivity to noise "Spacing out," phobic behavior, cognitive confusion, regressive behaviors, anxious attachment, sadness, helplessness, sense of foreshortened future Sleeplessness, tantrums, acting out, inattention to instructions, sensitivity to auditory stimuli; exaggerated startle response	Recurrent revenge/rescue fantasies, nightmares, night terrors, intrusive images, trauma reenactment, fears, somatic complaints "Spacing out," phobias, time skew, omen formation, school refusal, withdrawal, lack of interest in play, sadness, guilt, loneliness, futurelessness Difficulty sleeping, academic difficulties, oppositionality, obsession with trauma details, exaggerated startle response	Repetitive play, nightmares, intrusive images, trauma reenactment, separation anxiety, stranger anxiety, regressive fears, eating problems, sensitivity to noise "Spacing out," phobic behavior, cognitive confusion, regression, anxious attachment, sadness, helplessness, futurelessness Difficulty sleeping, tantrums, acting out, inattention to instructions, sensitivity to auditory stimuli; exaggerated startle response	Recurrent recollections, distressing dreams, feeling that event is recurring, distress when exposed to traumatic cues Avoidance of thoughts, feelings people, places, activities; inability to recall event, diminished interest in activities, detachment from others, restricted range of affect, sense of foreshortened future Insomnia, irritability, anger, difficulty concentrating, hypervigilance, exaggerated startle response

(continues)

Table 3
Developmental Impact of Exposure to Maltreatment and Violence and Considerations for Intervention (*Continued*)

	Infancy/toddlerhood	Preschool age	School age	Early adolescence	Late adolescence/ emerging adulthood
Trauma processing	Dependent on caregivers to define experiences and provide safety. No defenses other than seeking comfort from caregiver; caregiver's response will determine outcome. Memories not cognitively labeled or organized but stored as experienced, accompanied by primary, intense, affects easily triggered by reminiscent sights, sounds, etc.	Trauma may appear to have fleeting impact because of child's labile emotions. Affective states develop into stable schema that is overgeneralized. Traumatic events and related affects conflated and distorted to all experiences. If trauma persists, autonomy likely to be disrupted; excessively controlling of self (internalizing) or environment (externalizing)	Use concrete operational skills to assimilate trauma, need to acquire info and details via repeated questioning. Able to experience multiple emotions and perspectives in mind, beginning of ambivalence. Thoughts/feelings regarding event experienced as sold "facts". Memories processed more realistically but thoughts and feelings experienced as solid "facts"	Disillusionment and moodiness when reality fails to match ideals	Outside of family of origin, a new chance for appraising past and ongoing experiences

	Limited ability to use language to mediate experience If trauma persists, effects pervade functioning; ability to form close relationships, manage dependency needs, communicate emotions			
Implications for intervention	Family context and parent–child relations key Therapy must be experiential rather than verbal	External reinforcement is key Must place symptoms like oppositionality in context of normative development	Facilitation of developmental mastery is key; involvement of peer group beneficial Can use concrete operational skills to assimilate trauma; focus on reducing distorted cognitions and negative appraisals	Youth-focused treatment recognizes need for independence from family and ownership of experience Group treatment provides powerful peer feedback	College screening and prevention (and, for former foster youth, independent living services) may allow for detection and referral to therapy Ongoing victimization within the family and in romantic relationships complicate recovery

Note. PTSD = posttraumatic stress disorder. Data from Connolly (2014); Duncan (2000); P. A. Fisher, Chamberlain, and Leve (2009); Foster, Hagan, and Brooks-Gunn (2008); Hyman, Gold, and Sinha (2010); Kerig (2003); Kerig et al. (2012); Margolin and Vickerman (2011); Osofsky and Lieberman (2011); Pynoos (1993); Racco and Vis (2015); Read, van Os, Morrison, and Ross (2005); Scheeringa, Zeanah, Drell, and Larrieu (1995); and Silberg (2013).

References

AARP. (n.d.). *GrandFacts*. Retrieved from http://www.aarp.org/relationships/friends-family/grandfacts-sheets

Abel, G. G., & Harlow, N. (2002). The Abel Harlow Child Molestation Prevention Study. Retrieved from http://www.cmrpi.org/pdfs/study.pdf

ACA Camp Crisis Hotline. (2012, October). *Annual review 2012*. Retrieved from http://www.acacamps.org/resource-library/articles/aca-camp-crisis-hotline-annual-review-2012

Acoca, L. (1999). Investing in girls: A 21st century strategy. *Juvenile Justice, 6*, 3–13.

Adamsbaum, C., Grabar, S., Mejean, N., & Rey-Salmon, C. (2010). Abusive head trauma: Judicial admissions highlight violent and repetitive shaking. *Pediatrics, 126*, 546–555. http://dx.doi.org/10.1542/peds.2009-3647

Ahrens, K. R., DuBois, D. L., Richardson, L. P., Fan, M.-Y., & Lozano, P. (2008). Youth in foster care with adult mentors during adolescence have improved adult outcomes. *Pediatrics, 121*, e246–e252.

Ainsworth, M. D. (1979). Infant–mother attachment. *American Psychologist, 34*, 932–937. http://dx.doi.org/10.1037/0003-066X.34.10.932

American Psychiatric Association. (2000). *Diagnostic and statistical manual of mental disorders* (4th ed.). Washington, DC: Author.

American Psychiatric Association. (2013). *Diagnostic and statistical manual of mental disorders* (5th ed.). Arlington, VA: Author.

Armstrong, J. G., Putnam, F. W., Carlson, E. B., Libero, D. Z., & Smith, S. R. (1997). Development and validation of a measure of adolescent dissociation: The Adolescent Dissociative Experiences Scale. *Journal of Nervous and Mental Disease, 185*, 491–497.

Arnett, J. J. (2000). Emerging adulthood: A theory of development from the late teens through the twenties. *American Psychologist, 55*, 469–480. http://dx.doi.org/10.1037/0003-066X.55.5.469

REFERENCES

Arnett, J. J. (2001). Conceptions of the transition to adulthood: Perspectives from adolescence through midlife. *Journal of Adult Development, 8,* 133–143. http://dx.doi.org/10.1023/A:1026450103225

Arnett, J. J. (2005). The developmental context of substance use in emerging adulthood. *Journal of Drug Issues, 35,* 235–254. http://dx.doi.org/10.1177/002204260503500202

Arnett, J. J. (2006). Emerging adulthood: Understanding the new way of coming of age. In J. J. Arnett & J. L. Tanner (Eds.), *Emerging adults in America: Coming of age in the 21st century* (pp. 3–19). Washington, DC: American Psychological Association.

Arnett, J. J. (2014). *Emerging adulthood: The winding road from the late teens through the twenties.* New York, NY: Oxford University Press. http://dx.doi.org/10.1093/acprof:oso/9780199929382.001.0001

Avery, R. J., & Freundlich, M. (2009). You're all grown up now: Termination of foster care support at age 18. *Journal of Adolescence, 32,* 247–257. http://dx.doi.org/10.1016/j.adolescence.2008.03.009

Bailey, S. J., Haynes, D. C., & Letiecq, B. L. (2013). "How can you retire when you still got a kid in school?": Economics of raising grandchildren in rural areas. *Marriage & Family Review, 49,* 671–693. http://dx.doi.org/10.1080/01494929.2013.803009

Ball, B., Kerig, P., & Rosenbluth, B. (2009). Like a family but better because you can actually trust each other. *Health Promotion Practice, 10*(Suppl. 1), 45S–58S. http://dx.doi.org/10.1177/1524839908322115

Ballon, B. C., Courbasson, C. M., & Smith, P. D. (2001). Physical and sexual abuse issues among youths with substance use problems. *Canadian Journal of Psychiatry, 46,* 617–621.

Barr, M. (n.d.). *Information for dads.* Retrieved from http://www.purplecrying.info/information-for-dads.php

Barr, R. G. (2012). Preventing abusive head trauma resulting from a failure of normal interaction between infants and their caregivers. *Proceedings of the National Academy of Sciences of the United States of America, 109*(Suppl. 2), 17294–17301. http://dx.doi.org/10.1073/pnas.1121267109

Barr, R. G., Barr, M., Fujiwara, T., Conway, J., Catherine, N., & Brant, R. (2009). Do educational materials change knowledge and behaviour about crying and shaken baby syndrome? A randomized controlled trial. *Canadian Medical Association Journal, 180,* 727–733. http://dx.doi.org/10.1503/cmaj.081419

Barr, R. G., Rivara, F. P., Barr, M., Cummings, P., Taylor, J., Lengua, L. J., & Meredith-Benitz, E. (2009). Effectiveness of educational materials designed to change knowledge and behaviors regarding crying and shaken-baby syn-

REFERENCES

drome in mothers of newborns: A randomized, controlled trial. *Pediatrics*, *123*, 972–980. http://dx.doi.org/10.1542/peds.2008-0908

Barr, R. G., Trent, R. B., & Cross, J. (2006). Age-related incidence curve of hospitalized shaken baby syndrome cases: Convergent evidence for crying as a trigger to shaking. *Child Abuse & Neglect*, *30*, 7–16. http://dx.doi.org/10.1016/j.chiabu.2005.06.009

Baumrind, D., Larzelere, R. E., & Owens, E. B. (2010). Effects of preschool parents' power assertive patterns and practices on adolescent development. *Parenting: Science and Practice*, *10*, 157–201. http://dx.doi.org/10.1080/15295190903290790

Becker-Blease, K. A., Finkelhor, D., & Turner, H. (2008). Media exposure predicts children's reactions to crime and terrorism. *Journal of Trauma & Dissociation*, *9*, 225–248. http://dx.doi.org/10.1080/15299730802048652

Becker-Blease, K. A., & Freyd, J. J. (2005). Beyond PTSD: An evolving relationship between trauma theory and family violence research. *Journal of Interpersonal Violence*, *20*, 403–411. http://dx.doi.org/10.1177/0886260504269485

Becker-Blease, K. A., & Freyd, J. J. (2008). A preliminary study of ADHD symptoms and correlates: Do abused children differ from nonabused children? *Journal of Aggression, Maltreatment & Trauma*, *17*, 133–140. http://dx.doi.org/10.1080/10926770802250736

Becker-Blease, K. A., Tucker, C. J., & Holt, M. (2008, December). *Family abuse, siblings, and the "age of possibilities"* (NCFR monthly report). Minneapolis, MN: National Council on Family Relations.

Beeghly, M., & Cicchetti, D. (1994). Child maltreatment, attachment, and the self system: Emergence of an internal state lexicon in toddlers at high social risk. *Development and Psychopathology*, *6*, 5–30. http://dx.doi.org/10.1017/S095457940000585X

Beitchman, J. H., Zucker, K. J., Hood, J. E., & DaCosta, G. A. (1992). A review of the long-term effects of child sexual abuse. *Child Abuse & Neglect*, *16*, 101–118.

Belsky, J., & Pluess, M. (2009). Beyond diathesis stress: Differential susceptibility to environmental influences. *Psychological Bulletin*, *135*, 885–908. http://dx.doi.org/10.1037/a0017376

Bennett, D. C., Kerig, P. K., Chaplo, S., McGee, A. B., & Baucom, B. R. (2014). Validation of the five-factor model of PTSD symptom structure among delinquent youth. *Psychological Trauma: Theory, Research, Practice, and Policy*, *6*, 438–447.

Biron, D., & Shelton, D. (2005). Perpetrator accounts in infant abusive head trauma brought about by a shaking event. *Child Abuse & Neglect*, *29*, 1347–1358. http://dx.doi.org/10.1016/j.chiabu.2005.05.003

REFERENCES

Blair, C., & Raver, C. C. (2012). Child development in the context of adversity: Experiential canalization of brain and behavior. *American Psychologist, 67,* 309–318. http://dx.doi.org/10.1037/a0027493

Blaustein, M. E., & Kinniburgh, K. M. (2010). *Treating traumatic stress in children and adolescents: How to foster resilience through attachment, self-regulation, and competency.* New York, NY: Guilford Press.

Blome, W. W. (1997). What happens to foster kids: Educational experiences of a random sample of foster care youth and a matched group of non-foster care youth. *Child & Adolescent Social Work Journal, 14,* 41–53. http://dx.doi.org/10.1023/A:1024592813809

Bowlby, J. (1951). Maternal care and mental health. *Bulletin of the World Health Organization, 3,* 355–533.

Bowlby, J. (1969). *Attachment and loss: Volume 1. Loss.* New York, NY: Basic Books.

Boyd, L. W. (2013). *Therapeutic foster care: Exceptional care for complex, trauma-impacted youth in foster care.* Retrieved from http://childwelfaresparc.org/wp-content/uploads/2014/07/11-therapeutic-foster-care-exceptional-care-for-complex-trauma-impacted-youth-in-foster-care.pdf

Boynton-Jarrett, R., Wright, R. J., Putnam, F. W., Lividoti Hibert, E., Michels, K. B., Forman, M. R., & Rich-Edwards, J. (2013). Childhood abuse and age at menarche. *Journal of Adolescent Health, 52,* 241–247. http://dx.doi.org/10.1016/j.jadohealth.2012.06.006

Brazelton, T. B., Tronick, E., Adamson, L., Als, H., & Wise, S. (1975). Early mother–infant reciprocity. *Ciba Foundation Symposium, 33,* 137–154.

Bretherton, I., Ridgeway, D., & Cassidy, J. (1990). Assessing internal working models of the attachment relationship. In M. T. Greenberg, D. Cicchetti, & E. M. Cummings (Eds.), *Attachment in the preschool years: Theory, research, and intervention* (pp. 273–308). Chicago, IL: University of Chicago Press.

Brezina, T. (1998). Adolescent maltreatment and delinquency: The question of intervening processes. *Journal of Research in Crime and Delinquency, 35,* 71–99.

Briere, J. (2010). *Trauma Symptom Inventory—2nd edition (TSI-2) professional manual.* Odessa, FL: Psychological Assessment Resources.

Briscoe-Smith, A. M., & Hinshaw, S. P. (2006). Linkages between child abuse and attention-deficit/hyperactivity disorder in girls: Behavioral and social correlates. *Child Abuse & Neglect, 30,* 1239–1255. http://dx.doi.org/10.1016/j.chiabu.2006.04.008

Brodsky, B. S., Mann, J. J., Stanley, B., Tin, A., Oquendo, M., Birmaher, B., . . . Burke, A. K. (2008). Familial transmission of suicidal behavior: Factors mediating the relationship between childhood abuse and offspring suicide attempts. *The Journal of Clinical Psychiatry, 69,* 584–596.

REFERENCES

Bucharest Early Intervention Project. (n.d.). Retrieved from http://www.bucharestearlyinterventionproject.org/index.html

Burnette, M. L., Oshri, A., Lax, R., Richards, D., & Ragbeer, S. N. (2012). Pathways from harsh parenting to adolescent antisocial behavior: A multidomain test of gender moderation. *Development and Psychopathology, 24,* 857–870. http://dx.doi.org/10.1017/S0954579412000417

Bush, N., & Boyce, W. T. (2014). The Contributions of Early Experience to Biological Development and Sensitivity to Context. In M. Lewis & K. D. Rudolph (Eds.), *Handbook of developmental psychopathology* (pp. 287–309). New York, NY: Springer. http://dx.doi.org/10.1007/978-1-4614-9608-3_15

Casey Family Programs. (n.d.). *Ansell-Casey Life Skills Assessment.* Retrieved from http://lifeskills.casey.org

Cauffman, E. (2008). Understanding the female offender. *The Future of Children, 18,* 119–142.

Cavanagh, S. E. (2004). The sexual debut of girls in early adolescence: The intersection of race, pubertal timing, and friendship group characteristics. *Journal of Research on Adolescence, 14,* 285–312. http://dx.doi.org/10.1111/j.1532-7795.2004.00076.x

Centers for Disease Control and Prevention. (2012). *Cost of child abuse and neglect rival other major public health problems.* Retrieved from http://www.cdc.gov/violenceprevention/childmaltreatment/economiccost.html

Cernkovich, S. A., Lanctôt, N., & Giordano, P. C. (2008). Predicting adolescent and adult antisocial behavior among adjudicated delinquent females. *Crime & Delinquency, 54,* 3–33.

Chaffin, M., Letourneau, E., & Silovsky, J. F. (2002). Adults, adolescents, and children who sexually abuse children: A developmental perspective. In J. E. B. Myers, L. Berliner, J. Briere, C. T. Hendrix, C. Jenny, & T. A. Reid (Eds.), *The APSAC handbook on child maltreatment* (2nd ed., pp. 205–232). Thousand Oaks, CA: Sage.

Chang, L., Schwartz, D., Dodge, K. A., & McBride-Chang, C. (2003). Harsh parenting in relation to child emotion regulation and aggression. *Journal of Family Psychology, 17,* 598–606.

Chaplo, S. D., Kerig, P. K., Bennett, D. C., & Modrowski, C. A. (2015). The roles of emotion dysregulation and dissociation in the association between sexual abuse and self-injury among juvenile justice-involved youth. *Journal of Trauma & Dissociation, 16,* 272–285. http://dx.doi.org/10.1080/15299732.2015.989647

Chard, K. M. (2005). An evaluation of cognitive processing therapy for the treatment of posttraumatic stress disorder related to childhood sexual abuse. *Journal of Consulting and Clinical Psychology, 73,* 965–971.

REFERENCES

Chesney-Lind, M., & Belknap, J. (2004). Trends in delinquent girls' aggression and violent behavior: A review of the evidence. In M. Putallaz & K. L. Bierman (Eds.), *Aggression, antisocial behavior, and violence among girls* (pp. 203–220). New York, NY: Guilford Press.

Chesney-Lind, M., & Pasko, L. (2004). *The female offender: Girls, women, and crime.* Thousand Oaks, CA: Sage.

Child Welfare Information Gateway. (2013a). *Alternatives for families: A cognitive-behavioral therapy (AF–CBT).* Washington, DC: U.S. Department of Health and Human Services, & Children's Bureau. Retrieved from https://www.childwelfare.gov/pubs/cognitive

Child Welfare Information Gateway. (2013b). *Siblings issues in foster care and adoption.* Washington, DC: U.S. Department of Health and Human Services, & Children's Bureau. Retrieved from https://www.childwelfare.gov/pubs/siblingissues/siblingissues.pdf

Chisholm, J. S., Quinlivan, J. A., Petersen, R. W., & Coall, D. A. (2005). Early stress predicts age at menarche and first birth, adult attachment, and expected lifespan. *Human Nature, 16,* 233–265. http://dx.doi.org/10.1007/s12110-005-1009-0

Cicchetti, D. (1991). Fractures in the crystal: Developmental psychopathology and the emergence of self. *Developmental Review, 11,* 271–287. http://dx.doi.org/10.1016/0273-2297(91)90014-F

Cicchetti, D., Rogosch, F. A., Maughan, A., Toth, S. L., & Bruce, J. (2003). False belief understanding in maltreated children. *Development and Psychopathology, 15,* 1067–1091. http://dx.doi.org/10.1017/S0954579403000440

Cicchetti, D., & Toth, S. L. (1995). A developmental psychopathology perspective on child abuse and neglect. *Journal of the American Academy of Child & Adolescent Psychiatry, 34,* 541–565. http://dx.doi.org/10.1097/00004583-199505000-00008

Cicchetti, D., & Toth, S. L. (1998). The development of depression in children and adolescents. *American Psychologist, 53,* 221–241. http://dx.doi.org/10.1037/0003-066X.53.2.221

Cicchetti, D., & Toth, S. L. (2005). Child maltreatment. *Annual Review of Clinical Psychology, 1,* 409–438. http://dx.doi.org/10.1146/annurev.clinpsy.1.102803.144029

Cicchetti, D., & Valentino, K. (2006). An ecological-transactional perspective on child maltreatment: Failure of the average expectable environment and its influence on child development. In D. Cicchetti & D. J. Cohen (Eds.), *Developmental psychopathology: Volume III. Risk, disorder and adaptation* (2nd ed., pp. 129–201). New York, NY: Wiley.

Cohen, J. A., Deblinger, E., Mannarino, A. P., & Steer, R. A. (2004). A multisite, randomized controlled trial for children with sexual abuse-related PTSD symptoms. *Journal of the American Academy of Child & Adolescent Psychiatry, 43*, 393–402. http://dx.doi.org/10.1097/00004583-200404000-00005

Cohen, J. A., Mannarino, A. P., & Deblinger, E. (2006). *Treating trauma and traumatic grief in children and adolescents.* New York, NY: Guilford Press.

Cohen, J. A., Mannarino, A. P., & Deblinger, E. (2012). *Trauma-focused CBT for children and adolescents: Treatment applications.* New York, NY: Guilford Press.

Cohen, L. J., & Galynker, I. I. (2002). Clinical features of pedophilia and implications for treatment. *Journal of Psychiatric Practice, 8*, 276–289. http://dx.doi.org/10.1097/00131746-200209000-00004

Cohen, P., Smailes, E., & Brown, J. (2004). Effects of childhood maltreatment on adult arrests in a general population sample. In B. S. Fisher (Ed.), *Violence against women and family violence: Developments in research, practice, and policy* (pp. II-1–10). Washington, DC: National Institute of Justice, Office of Justice Programs, U.S. Department of Justice.

Cole, P. M., & Putnam, F. W. (1992). Effect of incest on self and social functioning: A developmental psychopathology perspective. *Journal of Consulting and Clinical Psychology, 60*, 174–184. http://dx.doi.org/10.1037/0022-006X.60.2.174

Cole, S. F., Eisner, A., Gregory, M., & Ristuccia, J. (2013). *Helping traumatized children learn: Volume 2. Creating and advocating for trauma-sensitive schools.* Boston, MA: Massachusetts Advocates for Children, Trauma and Learning Policy Initiative.

Cole, S. F., Greenwald O'Brien, J., Gadd, M. G., Ristuccia, J., Wallace, D. L., & Gregory, M. (2005). *Helping traumatized children learn: Vol. 1. A report and policy agenda.* Boston, MA: Massachusetts Advocates for Children, Trauma and Learning Policy Initiative.

Colvert, E., Rutter, M., Kreppner, J., Beckett, C., Castle, J., Groothues, C., . . . Sonuga-Barke, E. J. (2008). Do theory of mind and executive function deficits underlie the adverse outcomes associated with profound early deprivation? Findings from the English and Romanian adoptees study. *Journal of Abnormal Child Psychology, 36*, 1057–1068. http://dx.doi.org/10.1007/s10802-008-9232-x

Connolly, J. (2014). Outcomes in emerging adulthood for maltreated youth: A clinical-developmental approach. *Child Maltreatment, 19*, 270–274. http://dx.doi.org/10.1177/1077559514557932

Courtois, C. A., & Gold, S. N. (2009). The need for inclusion of psychological trauma in the professional curriculum: A call to action. *Psychological Trauma: Theory, Research, Practice, and Policy, 1*, 3–23.

Crittenden, P. M. (1992). Quality of attachment in the preschool years. *Development and Psychopathology, 4*, 209–241. http://dx.doi.org/10.1017/S095457 9400000110

Crittenden, P. M. (1999). Atypical attachment in infancy and early childhood among children at developmental risk. VII. Danger and development: The organization of self-protective strategies. *Monographs of the Society for Research in Child Development, 64*, 145–171. http://dx.doi.org/10.1111/1540-5834.00037

Crittenden, P. M., & DiLalla, D. L. (1988). Compulsive compliance: The development of an inhibitory coping strategy in infancy. *Journal of Abnormal Child Psychology, 16*, 585–599. http://dx.doi.org/10.1007/BF00914268

Cross, T. P., Jones, L. M., Walsh, W. A., Simone, M., Kolko, D. J., Szczepanski, J., . . . Magnuson, S. (2008, August). Evaluating children's advocacy centers' response to child sexual abuse. *Juvenile Justice Bulletin*, 1–12. Retrieved from https://www.ncjrs.gov/pdffiles1/ojjdp/218530.pdf

Culp, R. E., Watkins, R. V., Lawrence, H., Letts, D., Kelly, D. J., & Rice, M. L. (1991). Maltreated children's language and speech development: Abused, neglected, and abused and neglected. *First Language, 11*, 377–389. http://dx.doi.org/10.1177/014272379101103305

Cupoli, J. M., & Sewell, P. M. (1988). One thousand fifty-nine children with a chief complaint of sexual abuse. *Child Abuse & Neglect, 12*, 151–162. http://dx.doi.org/10.1016/0145-2134(88)90023-3

Cyr, M., McDuff, P., & Wright, J. (2006). Prevalence and predictors of dating violence among adolescent female victims of child sexual abuse. *Journal of Interpersonal Violence, 21*, 1000–1017.

Davis, J. L., & Petretic-Jackson, P. A. (2000). The impact of child sexual abuse on adult interpersonal functioning: A review and synthesis of the empirical literature. *Aggression and Violent Behavior, 5*, 291–328. http://dx.doi.org/10.1016/S1359-1789(99)00010-5

De Bellis, M. D. (2001). Developmental traumatology: The psychobiological development of maltreated children and its implications for research, treatment, and policy. *Development and Psychopathology, 13*, 539–564. http://dx.doi.org/10.1017/S0954579401003078

Deblinger, E., Mannarino, A. P., Cohen, J. A., & Steer, R. A. (2006). A follow-up study of a multisite, randomized, controlled trial for children with sexual abuse-related PTSD symptoms. *Journal of the American Academy of Child & Adolescent Psychiatry, 45*, 1474–1484. http://dx.doi.org/10.1097/01.chi.0000240839.56114.bb

Delker, B. C., & Freyd, J. J. (2014). From betrayal to the bottle: Investigating possible pathways from trauma to problematic substance use. *Journal of Traumatic Stress, 27*, 576–584. http://dx.doi.org/10.1002/jts.21959

DePrince, A. P., & Newman, E. (2011). The art and science of trauma-focused training and education. *Psychological Trauma, 3*, 13–14.

Dias, M. S., Smith, K., DeGuehery, K., Mazur, P., Li, V., & Shaffer, M. L. (2005). Preventing abusive head trauma among infants and young children: A hospital-based, parent education program. *Pediatrics, 115*, e470–e477. http://dx.doi.org/10.1542/peds.2004-1896

Dierkhising, C. B., Ko, S. J., Woods-Jaeger, B., Briggs, E. C., Lee, R., & Pynoos, R. S. (2013). Trauma histories among justice-involved youth: findings from the National Child Traumatic Stress Network. *European Journal of Psychotraumatology, 4*. http://dx.doi.org/10.3402/ejpt.v4i0.20274

Dodge, K. A., & Pettit, G. S. (2003). A biopsychosocial model of the development of chronic conduct problems in adolescence. *Developmental Psychology, 39*, 349–371. http://dx.doi.org/10.1037/0012-1649.39.2.349

Dubé, R., & Hébert, M. (1988). Sexual abuse of children under 12 years of age: A review of 511 cases. *Child Abuse & Neglect, 12*, 321–330. http://dx.doi.org/10.1016/0145-2134(88)90045-2

DuBois, D. L., Portillo, N., Rhodes, J. E., Silverthorn, N., & Valentine, J. C. (2011). How effective are mentoring programs for youth? A systematic assessment of the evidence. *Psychological Science in the Public Interest, 12*, 57–91.

Duncan, R. D. (2000). Childhood maltreatment and college drop-out rates: Implications for child abuse researchers. *Journal of Interpersonal Violence, 15*, 987–995. http://dx.doi.org/10.1177/088626000015009005

Egeland, B., Bosquet, M., & Chung, A. L. (2002). Continuities and discontinuities in the intergenerational transmission of child maltreatment: Implications for breaking the cycle of abuse. In K. D. Browne, H. Hanks, P. Stratton, & C. Hamilton-Giachritsis (Eds.), *Early prediction and prevention of child abuse: A handbook* (pp. 217–232). Chichester, England: Wiley.

Egeland, B., Yates, T., Appleyard, K., & van Dulmen, M. (2002). The long-term consequences of maltreatment in the early years: A developmental pathway model to antisocial behavior. *Children's Services: Social Policy, Research, & Practice, 5*, 249–260. http://dx.doi.org/10.1207/s15326918cs0504_2

Ehrensaft, M. K., Cohen, P., Brown, J., Smailes, E., Chen, H., & Johnson, J. G. (2003). Intergenerational transmission of partner violence: A 20-year prospective study. *Journal of Consulting and Clinical Psychology, 71*, 741–752. http://dx.doi.org/10.1037/0022-006X.71.4.741

Ellingson, K. D., Leventhal, J. M., & Weiss, H. B. (2008). Using hospital discharge data to track inflicted traumatic brain injury. *American Journal of Preventive Medicine, 34*(Suppl. 4), S157–S162. http://dx.doi.org/10.1016/j.amepre.2007.12.021

REFERENCES

Elliott, M., Browne, K., & Kilcoyne, J. (1995). Child sexual abuse prevention: What offenders tell us. *Child Abuse & Neglect, 19,* 579–594. http://dx.doi.org/10.1016/0145-2134(95)00017-3

Ellis, B. J., & Boyce, W. T. (2008). Biological sensitivity to context. *Current Directions in Psychological Science, 17,* 183–187. http://dx.doi.org/10.1111/j.1467-8721.2008.00571.x

English, D., Widom, C., & Brandford, C. (2002). *Childhood victimization and delinquency, adult criminality, and violent criminal behavior: A replication and extension.* Washington, DC: National Institute of Justice.

Erickson, M. F., Sroufe, L. A., & Egeland, B. (1985). The relationship between quality of attachment and behavior problems in preschool in a high-risk sample. *Monographs of the Society for Research in Child Development, 50,* 147–166. http://dx.doi.org/10.2307/3333831

Evans, S. E., Davies, C., & DiLillo, D. (2008). Exposure to domestic violence: A meta-analysis of child and adolescent outcomes. *Aggression and Violent Behavior, 13,* 131–140. http://dx.doi.org/10.1016/j.avb.2008.02.005

Fang, X., Brown, D. S., Florence, C. S., & Mercy, J. A. (2012). The economic burden of child maltreatment in the United States and implications for prevention. *Child Abuse & Neglect, 36,* 156–165. http://dx.doi.org/10.1016/j.chiabu.2011.10.006

Feiring, C., Miller-Johnson, S., & Cleland, C. M. (2007). Potential pathways from stigmatization and internalizing symptoms to delinquency in sexually abused youth. *Child Maltreatment, 12,* 220–232.

Feiring, C., Simon, V. A., Cleland, C. M., & Barrett, E. P. (2013). Potential pathways from stigmatization and externalizing behavior to anger and dating aggression in sexually abused youth. *Journal of Clinical Child & Adolescent Psychology, 42,* 309–322. http://dx.doi.org/10.1080/15374416.2012.736083

Feiring, C., Taska, L., & Lewis, M. (2002). Adjustment following sexual abuse discovery: The role of shame and attributional style. *Developmental Psychology, 38,* 79–92.

Fergusson, D. M., Boden, J. M., & Horwood, L. J. (2008). Exposure to childhood sexual and physical abuse and adjustment in early adulthood. *Child Abuse & Neglect, 32,* 607–619. http://dx.doi.org/10.1016/j.chiabu.2006.12.018

Fergusson, D. M., McLeod, G. F. H., & Horwood, L. J. (2013). Childhood sexual abuse and adult developmental outcomes: Findings from a 30-year longitudinal study in New Zealand. *Child Abuse & Neglect, 37,* 664–674. http://dx.doi.org/10.1016/j.chiabu.2013.03.013

Finkelhor, D. (2007). Developmental victimology: The comprehensive study of childhood victimizations. In R. C. Davis, A. J. Lurigio, & S. Herman (Eds.), *Victims of crime* (3rd. ed., pp. 9–34). Thousand Oaks, CA: Sage.

REFERENCES

Finkelhor, D. (2013). Developmental victimology: The comprehensive study of child victimization. In R. C. Davis, A. J. Lurigio, & S. Herman (Eds.), *Victims of crime* (4th ed., pp. 75–106). Thousand Oaks, CA: Sage.

Finkelhor, D., & Dziuba-Leatherman, J. (1995). Victimization prevention programs: A national survey of children's exposure and reactions. *Child Abuse & Neglect, 19,* 129–139. http://dx.doi.org/10.1016/0145-2134 (94)00111-7

Finkelhor, D., Hamby, S., Turner, H., & Ormrod, R. (2011). *The Juvenile Victimization Questionnaire—2nd Revision (JVQ–R2).* Durham, NH: Crimes Against Children Research Center.

Finkelhor, D., Jones, L. M., Shattuck, A., & Saito, K. (2013). *Updated trends in child maltreatment, 2012.* Retrieved from Crimes Against Children Research Center website: http://www.unh.edu/ccrc/pdf/CV203_Updated%20trends%202012_Revised_2_20_14.pdf

Finkelhor, D., & Kendall-Tackett, K. (1997). A developmental perspective on the childhood impact of crime, abuse, and violent victimization. In D. Cicchetti & S. L. Toth (Eds.), *Developmental perspectives on trauma: Theory, research, and intervention* (pp. 1–32). Rochester, NY: University of Rochester Press.

Finkelhor, D., Ormrod, R. K., & Turner, H. A. (2007). Poly-victimization: A neglected component in child victimization. *Child Abuse & Neglect, 31,* 7–26. http://dx.doi.org/10.1016/j.chiabu.2006.06.008

Finkelhor, D., Turner, H., Ormrod, R., & Hamby, S. L. (2009). Violence, abuse, and crime exposure in a national sample of children and youth. *Pediatrics, 124,* 1411–1423. http://dx.doi.org/10.1542/peds.2009-0467

Finkelhor, D., Turner, H., Ormrod, R., & Hamby, S. L. (2010). Trends in childhood violence and abuse exposure: Evidence from 2 national surveys. *Archives of Pediatrics & Adolescent Medicine, 164,* 238–242. http://dx.doi.org/10.1001/archpediatrics.2009.283

Fisher, B. S., Cullen, F. T., & Turner, M. G. (2000). *The sexual victimization of college women. Research report.* Washington, DC: Bureau of Justice Statistics, National Institute of Justice. Retrieved from https://www.ncjrs.gov/pdffiles1/nij/182369.pdf

Fisher, P. A., Chamberlain, P., & Leve, L. D. (2009). Improving the lives of foster children through evidenced-based interventions. *Vulnerable Children and Youth Studies, 4,* 122–127. http://dx.doi.org/10.1080/17450120902887368

Fisher, P. A., & Kim, H. K. (2007). Intervention effects on foster preschoolers' attachment-related behaviors from a randomized trial. *Prevention Science, 8,* 161–170. http://dx.doi.org/10.1007/s11121-007-0066-5

REFERENCES

Fisher, P. A., Kim, H. K., & Pears, K. C. (2009). Effects of Multidimensional Treatment Foster Care for Preschoolers (MTFC–P) on reducing permanent placement failures among children with placement instability. *Children and Youth Services Review, 31,* 541–546. http://dx.doi.org/10.1016/j.childyouth.2008.10.012

Fisher, P. A., Stoolmiller, M., Gunnar, M. R., & Burraston, B. O. (2007). Effects of a therapeutic intervention for foster preschoolers on diurnal cortisol activity. *Psychoneuroendocrinology, 32,* 892–905. http://dx.doi.org/10.1016/j.psyneuen.2007.06.008

Fivush, R. (1994). Young children's event recall: Are memories constructed through discourse? *Consciousness and Cognition: An International Journal, 3,* 356–373. http://dx.doi.org/10.1006/ccog.1994.1020

Fivush, R. (2010). Speaking silence: The social construction of silence in autobiographical and cultural narratives. *Memory, 18,* 88–98. http://dx.doi.org/10.1080/09658210903029404

Fivush, R., Berlin, L. J., Sales, J. M., Mennuti-Washburn, J., & Cassidy, J. (2003). Functions of parent–child reminiscing about emotionally negative events. *Memory, 11,* 179–192. http://dx.doi.org/10.1080/741938209

Flannery, D. J., Rowe, D. C., & Gulley, B. L. (1993). Impact of pubertal status, timing, and age on adolescent sexual experience and delinquency. *Journal of Adolescent Research, 8,* 21–40. http://dx.doi.org/10.1177/074355489381003

Flavell, J. H. (1999). Cognitive development: Children's knowledge about the mind. *Annual Review of Psychology, 50,* 21–45. http://dx.doi.org/10.1146/annurev.psych.50.1.21

Ford, J. D., & Blaustein, M. E. (2013). Systemic self-regulation: A framework for trauma-informed services in residential juvenile justice programs. *Journal of Family Violence, 28,* 665–677.

Ford, J. D., & Courtois, C. A. (2009). Defining and understanding complex trauma and complex traumatic stress disorders. In C. A. Courtois & J. D. Ford (Eds.), *Treating complex traumatic stress disorders: An evidence-based guide* (pp. 13–30). New York, NY: Guilford Press.

Ford, J. D., & Hawke, J. (2012). Trauma affect regulation psychoeducation group and milieu intervention outcomes in juvenile detention facilities. *Journal of Aggression, Maltreatment & Trauma, 21,* 365–384. http://dx.doi.org/10.1080/10926771.2012.673538

Ford, J. D., Racusin, R., Ellis, C. G., Daviss, W. B., Reiser, J., Fleischer, A., & Thomas, J. (2000). Child maltreatment, other trauma exposure, and posttraumatic symptomatology among children with oppositional defiant and attention deficit hyperactivity disorders. *Child Maltreatment, 5,* 205–217. http://dx.doi.org/10.1177/1077559500005003001

REFERENCES

Ford, J. D., Steinberg, K. L., Hawke, J., Levine, J., & Zhang, W. (2012). Randomized trial comparison of emotion regulation and relational psychotherapies for PTSD with girls involved in delinquency. *Journal of Clinical Child and Adolescent Psychology, 41*, 27–37. http://dx.doi.org/10.1080/15374416.2012.632343

Foshee, V., & Langwick, S. (2004). *Safe dates: An adolescent dating abuse prevention curriculum.* Center City, MN: Hazelden.

Foster, H., Hagan, J., & Brooks-Gunn, J. (2008). Growing up fast: Stress exposure and subjective "weathering" in emerging adulthood. *Journal of Health and Social Behavior, 49*, 162–177. http://dx.doi.org/10.1177/002214650804900204

Foster Care Independence Act, Pub. L. No. 106-169, 113 Stat. 1882. (1999).

Freund, K., & Blanchard, R. (1986). The concept of courtship disorder. *Journal of Sex & Marital Therapy, 12*, 79–92. http://dx.doi.org/10.1080/00926238608415397

Freyd, J. (1996). *Betrayal trauma: The logic of forgetting childhood abuse.* Cambridge, MA: Harvard University Press.

Friedman, M. J. (2014). Literature on *DSM–5* and *ICD–11*. *PTSD Research Quarterly, 25*, 1–10.

Friedrich, W. N., Fisher, J. L., Dittner, C. A., Acton, R., Berliner, L., Butler, J., . . . Wright, J. (2001). Child Sexual Behavior Inventory: Normative, psychiatric, and sexual abuse comparisons. *Child Maltreatment, 6*, 37–49. http://dx.doi.org/10.1177/1077559501006001004

Friedrich, W. N., Grambsch, P., Broughton, D., Kuiper, J. & Beilke, R. L. (1991). Normative sexual behavior in children. *Pediatrics, 88*, 456–464.

Friedrich, W. N., Grambsch, P., Damon, L., Hewitt, S. K., Koverola, C., Lang, R. A., . . . Broughton, D. (1992). Child Sexual Behavior Inventory: Normative and clinical comparisons. *Psychological Assessment, 4*, 303–311. http://dx.doi.org/10.1037/1040-3590.4.3.303

Garmezy, N., Masten, A. S., Nordstrom, L., & Ferrarese, M. (1979). The nature of competence in normal and deviant children. *The Primary Prevention of Psychopathology, 3*, 23–43.

Gidycz, C. A., McNamara, J. R., & Edwards, K. M. (2006). Women's risk perception and sexual victimization: A review of the literature. *Aggression and Violent Behavior, 11*, 441–456. http://dx.doi.org/10.1016/j.avb.2006.01.004

Gil, D. G. (1970). *Violence against children: Physical child abuse in the United States.* Cambridge, MA: Harvard University Press.

Gilbert, D. (2007). *The surprising science of happiness.* Retrieved from http://www.ted.com/talks/dan_gilbert_asks_why_are_we_happy#t-1590

Gilbert, R., Widom, C. S., Browne, K., Fergusson, D., Webb, E., & Janson, S. (2009). Burden and consequences of child maltreatment in high-income countries. *The Lancet, 373*, 68–81.

REFERENCES

Glod, C. A., & Teicher, M. H. (1996). Relationship between early abuse, post-traumatic stress disorder, and activity levels in prepubertal children. *Journal of the American Academy of Child & Adolescent Psychiatry, 35,* 1384–1393. http://dx.doi.org/10.1097/00004583-199610000-00026

Gobin, R. L., & Freyd, J. J. (2009). Betrayal and revictimization: Preliminary findings. *Psychological Trauma: Theory, Research, Practice, and Policy, 1,* 242–257. http://dx.doi.org/10.1037/a0017469

Goldstein, A. L., Henriksen, C. A., Davidov, D. M., Kimber, M., Pitre, N. Y., & Afifi, T. O. (2013). Childhood maltreatment, alcohol use disorders, and treatment utilization in a national sample of emerging adults. *Journal of Studies on Alcohol and Drugs, 74,* 185–194. http://dx.doi.org/10.15288/jsad.2013.74.185

Grant, N., Hamer, M., & Steptoe, A. (2009). Social isolation and stress-related cardiovascular, lipid, and cortisol responses. *Annals of Behavioral Medicine, 37,* 29–37. http://dx.doi.org/10.1007/s12160-009-9081-z

Grasso, D. J., Saunders, B. E., Williams, L. M., Hanson, R., Smith, D. W., & Fitzgerald, M. M. (2013). Patterns of multiple victimization among maltreated children in Navy families. *Journal of Traumatic Stress, 26,* 597–604. http://dx.doi.org/10.1002/jts.21853

Grazioplene, R. G., DeYoung, C. G., Rogosch, F. A., & Cicchetti, D. (2013). A novel differential susceptibility gene: CHRNA4 and moderation of the effect of maltreatment on child personality. *Journal of Child Psychology and Psychiatry, 54,* 872–880.

Greene, R. W. (2014). *The explosive child: A new approach for understanding and parenting easily frustrated, chronically inflexible children* (rev. ed.). New York, NY: HarperCollins.

Gregg, C. R., & Hansen-Stamp, C. (2012). *Child sexual abuse: Liability issues revisited.* Retrieved from http://www.acacamps.org/campline/fall-2012/child-sexual-abuse

Grella, C. E., & Joshi, V. (2003). Treatment processes and outcomes among adolescents with a history of abuse who are in drug treatment. *Child Maltreatment, 8,* 7–18. http://dx.doi.org/10.1177/1077559502239610

Grinstead, L. N., Leder, S., Jensen, S., & Bond, L. (2003). Review of research on the health of caregiving grandparents. *Journal of Advanced Nursing, 44,* 318–326. http://dx.doi.org/10.1046/j.1365-2648.2003.02807.x

Grossman, J. B., & Rhodes, J. E. (2002). The test of time: Predictors and effects of duration in youth mentoring relationships. *American Journal of Community Psychology, 30,* 199–219.

Grossmann, K., Grossmann, K. E., Kindler, H., & Zimmermann, P. (2008). A wider view of attachment and exploration: The influence of mothers and fathers on the development of psychological security from infancy to young adulthood. In J. Cassidy & P. R. Shaver (Eds.), *Handbook of attachment: Theory, research, and clinical applications* (2nd ed., pp. 857–879). New York, NY: Guilford Press.

Hall, R. C. W., & Hall, R. C. W. (2007). A profile of pedophilia: Definition, characteristics of offenders, recidivism, treatment outcomes, and forensic issues. *Mayo Clinic Proceedings, 82*, 457–471. http://dx.doi.org/10.4065/82.4.457

Hart, S. N., Brassard, M. R., Davidson, H. A., Rivelis, E., Diaz, V., & Binggeli, N. J. (2011). Psychological maltreatment. In J. E. B. Myers (Ed.), *The APSAC handbook on child maltreatment* (3rd ed., pp. 221–227). Thousand Oaks, CA: Sage.

Hawkley, L. C., & Cacioppo, J. T. (2010). Loneliness matters: A theoretical and empirical review of consequences and mechanisms. *Annals of Behavioral Medicine, 40*, 218–227. http://dx.doi.org/10.1007/s12160-010-9210-8

Haynie, D. L., Giordano, P. C., Manning, W. D., & Longmore, M. A. (2005). Adolescent romantic relationships and delinquency involvement. *Criminology, 43*, 177–210.

Hayslip, B., Jr., & Smith, G. C. (Eds.). (2013). *Resilient grandparent caregivers: A strengths-based perspective.* New York, NY: Routledge/Taylor & Francis.

Herman, J. L. (1997). *Trauma and recovery.* New York, NY: Basic Books.

Herman-Giddens, M. E., Sandler, A. D., & Friedman, N. E. (1988). Sexual precocity in girls: An association with sexual abuse? *American Journal of Diseases of Children, 142*, 431–433. http://dx.doi.org/10.1001/archpedi.1988.02150040085025

Herrenkohl, R. C., Egolf, B. P., & Herrenkohl, E. C. (1997). Preschool antecedents of adolescent assaultive behavior: A longitudinal study. *American Journal of Orthopsychiatry, 67*, 422–432.

Herrera, V. M., & McCloskey, L. A. (2003). Sexual abuse, family violence, and female delinquency: Findings from a longitudinal study. *Violence and Victims, 18*, 319–334.

Herz, D. C., Ryan, J. P., & Bilchik, S. (2010). Challenges facing crossover youth: An examination of juvenile-justice decision making and recidivism. *Family Court Review, 48*, 305–321.

Hindle, D. (2000). Assessing children's perspectives on sibling placements in foster or adoptive homes. *Clinical Child Psychology and Psychiatry, 5*, 613–625. http://dx.doi.org/10.1177/1359104500005004014

Holt, S., Buckley, H., & Whelan, S. (2008). The impact of exposure to domestic violence on children and young people: A review of the literature. *Child Abuse & Neglect, 32*, 797–810. http://dx.doi.org/10.1016/j.chiabu.2008.02.004

Hughes, V. (2013, July 29). Detachment: How can scientists act ethically when they are studying the victims of a human tragedy, such as the Romanian orphans? *Aeon Magazine.* Retrieved from http://aeon.co/magazine/worldviews/can-research-on-romanian-orphans-be-ethical

Hunter, J. A., Figueredo, A. J., Malamuth, N. M., & Becker, J. V. (2003). Juvenile sex offenders: Toward the development of a typology. *Sexual Abuse: Journal of Research and Treatment, 15,* 27–48.

Hyman, S. M., Gold, S. N., & Sinha, R. (2010). Coping with stress and trauma in young adulthood. In J. E. Grant & M. N. Potenza (Eds.), *Young adult mental health* (pp. 143–157). New York, NY: Oxford University Press.

Ireland, T. O., Smith, C. A., & Thornberry, T. P. (2002). Developmental issues in the impact of child maltreatment on later delinquency and drug use. *Criminology, 40,* 359–400. http://dx.doi.org/10.1111/j.1745-9125.2002.tb00960.x

Iwaniec, D. (2006). *The emotionally abused and neglected child: Identification, assessment and intervention. A practice handbook* (2nd ed.). New York, NY: Wiley.

Kadushin, A., Martin, J. A., & McGloin, J. (1981). *Child abuse—An interactional event.* New York, NY: Columbia University Press.

Kaltiala-Heino, R., Kosunen, E., & Rimpelä, M. (2003). Pubertal timing, sexual behaviour and self-reported depression in middle adolescence. *Journal of Adolescence, 26,* 531–545. http://dx.doi.org/10.1016/S0140-1971(03)00053-8

Kaltiala-Heino, R., Rimpelä, M., Rissanen, A., & Rantanen, P. (2001). Early puberty and early sexual activity are associated with bulimic-type eating pathology in middle adolescence. *Journal of Adolescent Health, 28,* 346–352. http://dx.doi.org/10.1016/S1054-139X(01)00195-1

Kaufman, J., & Widom, C. S. (1999). Childhood victimization, running away, and delinquency. *Journal of Research in Crime and Delinquency, 36,* 347–370.

Kellogg, N., & the American Academy of Pediatrics Committee on Child Abuse and Neglect. (2005). The evaluation of sexual abuse in children. *Pediatrics, 116,* 506–512. http://dx.doi.org/10.1542/peds.2005-1336

Kerig, P. K. (2003). In search of protective processes for children exposed to interparental violence. *Journal of Emotional Abuse, 3,* 149–181. http://dx.doi.org/10.1300/J135v03n03_01

Kerig, P. K. (2014a). Introduction: For better or worse: Intimate relationships as sources of risk or resilience for girls' delinquency [introduction to Special Issue]. *Journal of Research on Adolescence, 24,* 1–11.

Kerig, P. K. (2014b). Maltreatment and trauma in adolescence: A time of heightened risk and potential resilience. *Traumatic StressPoints, 28,* 1–21.

Kerig, P. K., & Becker, S. P. (2010). From internalizing to externalizing: Theoretical models of the processes linking PTSD to juvenile delinquency. In S. J. Egan (Ed.), *Posttraumatic stress disorder (PTSD): Causes, symptoms and treatment* (pp. 1–46). Hauppauge, NY: Nova Science.

Kerig, P. K., & Becker, S. P. (2012). Trauma and girls' delinquency. In S. Miller, L. D. Leve, & P. K. Kerig (Eds.), *Delinquent girls: Contexts, relationships, and adaptation* (pp. 119–143). New York, NY: Springer.

Kerig, P. K., & Becker, S. P. (2015). Early abuse and neglect as risk factors for the development of criminal and antisocial behavior. In J. Morizot & L. Kazemian (Eds.), *The development of criminal and antisocial behavior: Theory, research, and practical applications* (pp. 181–199). New York, NY: Springer. http://dx.doi.org/10.1007/978-3-319-08720-7_12

Kerig, P. K., Ludlow, A., & Wenar, C. (2012). *Developmental psychopathology: From infancy through adolescence* (6th ed.). Maidenhead, England: McGraw-Hill.

Kerig, P. K., & Schulz, M. S. (2012). The transition from adolescence to adulthood: What lies beneath and what lies beyond. In P. K. Kerig, M. S. Schulz, & S. T. Hauser (Eds.), *Adolescence and beyond: Family processes in development* (pp. 3–12). New York, NY: Oxford University Press.

Kerig, P. K., Vanderzee, K. L., Becker, S. P., & Ward, R. M. (2013). Deconstructing PTSD: Traumatic experiences, posttraumatic symptom clusters, and mental health problems among delinquent youth. In P. K. Kerig (Ed.), *Psychological trauma and juvenile delinquency* (pp. 47–62). London, England: Routledge.

Keyes, K. M., Eaton, N. R., Krueger, R. F., McLaughlin, K. A., Wall, M. M., Grant, B. F., & Hasin, D. S. (2012). Childhood maltreatment and the structure of common psychiatric disorders. *The British Journal of Psychiatry, 200*, 107–115. http://dx.doi.org/10.1192/bjp.bp.111.093062

Kim, J., Cicchetti, D., Rogosch, F. A., & Manly, J. T. (2009). Child maltreatment and trajectories of personality and behavioral functioning: Implications for the development of personality disorder. *Development and psychopathology, 21*, 889–912. http://dx.doi.org/10.1017/s0954579409000480

Kim-Cohen, J., Caspi, A., Taylor, A., Williams, B., Newcombe, R., Craig, I. W., & Moffitt, T. E. (2006). MAOA, maltreatment, and gene–environment interaction predicting children's mental health: New evidence and a meta-analysis. *Molecular Psychiatry, 11*, 903–913. http://dx.doi.org/10.1038/sj.mp.4001851

King, W. J., MacKay, M., Sirnick, A., & the Canadian Shaken Baby Study Group. (2003). Shaken baby syndrome in Canada: Clinical characteristics and outcomes of hospital cases. *Canadian Medical Association Journal, 168*, 155–159.

Kisiel, C. L., & Lyons, J. S. (2001). Dissociation as a mediator of psychopathology among sexually abused children and adolescents. *The American Journal of Psychiatry, 158*, 1034–1039. http://dx.doi.org/10.1176/appi.ajp.158.7.1034

Kothari, B. H., McBeath, B., Lamson-Siu, E., Webb, S. J., Sorenson, P., Bowen, H., . . . Bank, L. (2014). Development and feasibility of a sibling intervention for youth in foster care. *Evaluation and Program Planning, 47*, 91–99. http://dx.doi.org/10.1016/j.evalprogplan.2014.08.006

REFERENCES

Kruczek, T., & Vitanza, S. (2015). Posttraumatic stress disorder. In T. P. Gullotta, R. W. Plant, & M. A. Evans (Eds.), *Handbook of adolescent behavioral problems* (pp. 131–150). New York, NY: Springer.

Lansford, J. E., Dodge, K. A., Pettit, G. S., & Bates, J. E. (2010). Does physical abuse in early childhood predict substance use in adolescence and early adulthood? *Child Maltreatment, 15,* 190–194. http://dx.doi.org/10.1177/1077559509352359

Lansford, J. E., Dodge, K. A., Pettit, G. S., Bates, J. E., Crozier, J., & Kaplow, J. (2002). A 12-year prospective study of the long-term effects of early child physical maltreatment on psychological, behavioral, and academic problems in adolescence. *Archives of Pediatrics & Adolescent Medicine, 156,* 824–830. http://dx.doi.org/10.1001/archpedi.156.8.824

Larose, S., Bernier, A., & Tarabulsy, G. M. (2005). Attachment state of mind, learning dispositions, and academic performance during the college transition. *Developmental Psychology, 41,* 281–289.

Lee, C., Barr, R. G., Catherine, N., & Wicks, A. (2007). Age-related incidence of publicly reported shaken baby syndrome cases: Is crying a trigger for shaking? *Journal of Developmental and Behavioral Pediatrics, 28,* 288–293. http://dx.doi.org/10.1097/DBP.0b013e3180327b55

Lemon, K., Hines, A. M., & Merdinger, J. (2005). From foster care to young adulthood: The role of independent living programs in supporting successful transitions. *Children and Youth Services Review, 27,* 251–270. http://dx.doi.org/10.1016/j.childyouth.2004.09.005

Leslie, L. K., Stallone, K. A., Weckerly, J., McDaniel, A. L., & Monn, A. (2006). Implementing ADHD guidelines in primary care: Does one size fit all? *Journal of Health Care for the Poor and Underserved, 17,* 302–327. http://dx.doi.org/10.1353/hpu.2006.0064

Leve, L. D., Harold, G. T., Chamberlain, P., Landsverk, J. A., Fisher, P. A., & Vostanis, P. (2012). Practitioner review: Children in foster care—vulnerabilities and evidence-based interventions that promote resilience processes. *Journal of Child Psychology and Psychiatry, 53,* 1197–1211. http://dx.doi.org/10.1111/j.1469-7610.2012.02594.x

Levendosky, A. A., Huth-Bocks, A. C., Semel, M. A., & Shapiro, D. L. (2002). Trauma symptoms in preschool-age children exposed to domestic violence. *Journal of Interpersonal Violence, 17,* 150–164. http://dx.doi.org/10.1177/0886260502017002003

Leventhal, J. M., Martin, K. D., & Asnes, A. G. (2008). Incidence of fractures attributable to abuse in young hospitalized children: Results from analysis of a United States database. *Pediatrics, 122,* 599–604. http://dx.doi.org/10.1542/peds.2007-1959

Leventhal, J. M., Martin, K. D., & Asnes, A. G. (2010). Fractures and traumatic brain injuries: Abuse versus accidents in a US database of hospitalized children. *Pediatrics, 126*, e104–e115. http://dx.doi.org/10.1542/peds.2009-1076

Lieberman, A. F., Ghosh Ippen, C., & Van Horn, P. (2006). Child–parent psychotherapy: 6-month follow-up of a randomized controlled trial. *Journal of the American Academy of Child & Adolescent Psychiatry, 45*, 913–918. http://dx.doi.org/10.1097/01.chi.0000222784.03735.92

Lieberman, A. F., & Knorr, K. (2007). The impact of trauma: A developmental framework for infancy and early childhood. *Psychiatric Annals, 36*, 209–215. http://dx.doi.org/10.3928/0090-4481-20070401-10

Lieberman, A. F., Van Horn, P., & Ippen, C. G. (2005). Toward evidence-based treatment: Child-parent psychotherapy with preschoolers exposed to marital violence. *Journal of the American Academy of Child & Adolescent Psychiatry, 44*, 1241–1248. http://dx.doi.org/10.1097/01.chi.0000181047.59702.58

Linares, L. O., Li, M., Shrout, P. E., Brody, G. H., & Pettit, G. S. (2007). Placement shift, sibling relationship quality, and child outcomes in foster care: A controlled study. *Journal of Family Psychology, 21*, 736–743. http://dx.doi.org/10.1037/0893-3200.21.4.736

Lyons-Ruth, K., Alpern, L., & Repacholi, B. (1993). Disorganized infant attachment classification and maternal psychosocial problems as predictors of hostile-aggressive behavior in the preschool classroom. *Child Development, 64*, 572–585. http://dx.doi.org/10.2307/1131270

Main, M., & Solomon, J. (1990). Procedures for identifying infants as disorganized/disoriented during the Ainsworth Strange Situation. In M. T. Greenberg, D. Cicchetti, & E. M. Cummings (Eds.), *Attachment in the preschool years: Theory, research, and intervention* (pp. 121–160). Chicago, IL: University of Chicago Press.

Maltz, W. (2012). *Sexual healing journey* (3rd ed.). New York, NY: William Morrow Paperbacks.

Margolin, G., & Vickerman, K. A. (2011). Posttraumatic stress in children and adolescents exposed to family violence: I. Overview and issues. *Couple and Family Psychology: Research and Practice, 1*(S), 63–73. http://dx.doi.org/10.1037/2160-4096.1.S.63

Marrow, M. T., Knudsen, K. J., Olafson, E., & Bucher, S. E. (2013). The value of implementing TARGET within a trauma-informed juvenile justice setting. In P. K. Kerig (Ed.), *Psychological trauma and juvenile delinquency* (pp. 174–187). London, England: Routledge.

Marshall, N. A. (2012). A clinician's guide to recognizing and reporting parental psychological maltreatment of children. *Professional Psychology: Research and Practice, 43*, 73–79. http://dx.doi.org/10.1037/a0026677

REFERENCES

Massat, C. R., & Lundy, M. (1998). "Reporting costs" to nonoffending parents in cases of intrafamilial child sexual abuse. *Child Welfare: Journal of Policy, Practice, and Program, 77,* 371–388.

Masten, A. S. (2001). Ordinary magic: Resilience processes in development. *American Psychologist, 56,* 227–238.

Masten, A. S. (2014). *Ordinary magic: Resilience in development.* New York, NY: Guilford Press.

Masten, A. S., & Coatsworth, J. D. (1998). The development of competence in favorable and unfavorable environments: Lessons from research on successful children. *American Psychologist, 53,* 205–220. http://dx.doi.org/10.1037/0003-066X.53.2.205

Masten, A. S., Obradović, J., & Burt, K. B. (2006). Resilience in emerging adulthood: Developmental perspectives on continuity and transformation. In J. J. Arnett & J. L. Tanner (Eds.), *Emerging adults in America: Coming of age in the 21st century* (pp. 173–190). Washington, DC: American Psychological Association. http://dx.doi.org/10.1037/11381-007

Masten, A. S., & Tellegen, A. (2012). Resilience in developmental psychopathology: Contributions of the Project Competence Longitudinal Study. *Development and Psychopathology, 24,* 345–361. http://dx.doi.org/10.1017/S095457941200003X

Masten, A. S., & Wright, M. O. D. (1998). Cumulative risk and protection models of child maltreatment. *Journal of Aggression, Maltreatment & Trauma, 2,* 7–30. http://dx.doi.org/10.1300/J146v02n01_02

Matulis, S., Resick, P. A., Rosner, R., & Steil, R. (2013). Developmentally adapted cognitive processing therapy for adolescents suffering from posttraumatic stress disorder after childhood sexual or physical abuse: A pilot study. *Clinical Child and Family Psychology Review, 17,* 1–18.

McGee, R. A., Wolfe, D. A., & Wilson, S. K. (1997). Multiple maltreatment experiences and adolescent behavior problems: Adolescents' perspectives. *Development and Psychopathology, 9,* 131–150.

McGee, S. A., & Holmes, C. C. (2011). Treatment considerations with sexually traumatized adolescents. In P. Goodyear-Brown (Ed.), *Handbook of child sexual abuse: Identification, assessment, and treatment* (pp. 447–468). New York, NY: Wiley.

Mehta, D., Klengel, T., Conneely, K. N., Smith, A. K., Altmann, A., Pace, T. W., . . . Binder, E. B. (2013). Childhood maltreatment is associated with distinct genomic and epigenetic profiles in posttraumatic stress disorder. *Proceedings of the National Academy of Sciences of the United States of America, 110,* 8302–8307. http://dx.doi.org/10.1073/pnas.1217750110

Miller, S. A. (2012). *Theory of mind: Beyond the preschool years.* New York, NY: Psychology Press.

Millwood, M. (2011). Empathic understanding in couples with a female survivor of childhood sexual abuse. *Journal of Couple & Relationship Therapy, 10,* 327–344. http://dx.doi.org/10.1080/15332691.2011.613310

Moffitt, T. E. (2013). Childhood exposure to violence and lifelong health: Clinical intervention science and stress-biology research join forces. *Development and Psychopathology, 25,* 1619–1634. http://dx.doi.org/10.1017/S0954579413000801

Montgomery, M. J. (2005). Psychosocial intimacy and identity: From early adolescence to emerging adulthood. *Journal of Adolescent Research, 20,* 346–374. http://dx.doi.org/10.1177/0743558404273118

Moss, E., & Gosselin, C. (1997). Attachment and joint problem-solving experiences during the preschool period. *Social Development, 6,* 1–17. http://dx.doi.org/10.1111/j.1467-9507.1997.tb00091.x

MTA Cooperative Group. (1999). A 14-month randomized clinical trial of treatment strategies for attention-deficit/hyperactivity disorder. *Archives of General Psychiatry, 56,* 1073–1086. http://dx.doi.org/10.1001/archpsyc.56.12.1073

Mulsow, M. H., O'Neal, K. K., & Murry, V. M. (2001). Adult attention deficit hyperactivity disorder, the family, and child maltreatment. *Trauma, Violence, & Abuse, 2,* 36–50. http://dx.doi.org/10.1177/1524838001002001002

Najavits, L. M. (2002). *Seeking safety: A treatment manual for PTSD and substance abuse.* New York, NY: Guilford Press.

National Child Traumatic Stress Network. (n.d.). *Children and domestic violence.* Retrieved from http://www.nctsn.org/content/children-and-domestic-violence

National Sexual Violence Resource Center. (2011). *Child sexual abuse prevention: Programs for children.* Retrieved from http://www.nsvrc.org/sites/default/files/Publications_NSVRC_Guide_Child-Sexual-Abuse-Prevention-programs-for-children.pdf

Naylor, R., Breen, J., & Myers, K. (1999). *High Risk Infants Service Quality Initiatives Project: Development and early implementation report July 1997 to June 1999.* Melbourne, Australia: Victorian Government Department of Human Services.

Negriff, S., Noll, J. G., Shenk, C. E., Putnam, F. W., & Trickett, P. K. (2010). Associations between nonverbal behaviors and subsequent sexual attitudes and behaviors of sexually abused and comparison girls. *Child Maltreatment, 15,* 180–189.

Negriff, S., Schneiderman, J. U., Smith, C., Schreyer, J. K., & Trickett, P. K. (2014). Characterizing the sexual abuse experiences of young adolescents. *Child Abuse & Neglect, 38,* 261–270. http://dx.doi.org/10.1016/j.chiabu.2013.08.021

Nelson, C. A., III, Zeanah, C. H., Fox, N. A., Marshall, P. J., Smyke, A. T., & Guthrie, D. (2007). Cognitive recovery in socially deprived young children:

REFERENCES

The Bucharest Early Intervention Project. *Science*, *318*, 1937–1940. http://dx.doi.org/10.1126/science.1143921

Nelson, K., & Fivush, R. (2004). The emergence of autobiographical memory: A social cultural developmental theory. *Psychological Review*, *111*, 486–511. http://dx.doi.org/10.1037/0033-295X.111.2.486

Neumann, D. A., Houskamp, B. M., Pollock, V. E., & Briere, J. (1996). The long-term sequelae of childhood sexual abuse in women: A meta-analytic review. *Child Maltreatment*, *1*, 6–16. http://dx.doi.org/10.1177/1077559596001001002

Nigg, J. T. (2010). Attention-deficit/hyperactivity disorder endophenotypes, structure, and etiological pathways. *Current Directions in Psychological Science*, *19*, 24–29. http://dx.doi.org/10.1177/0963721409359282

Nock, M. K. (2010). Self-injury. *Annual Review of Clinical Psychology*, *6*, 339–363. http://dx.doi.org/10.1146/annurev.clinpsy.121208.131258

Noll, J. G., & Grych, J. H. (2011). Read–react–respond: An integrative model for understanding sexual revictimization. *Psychology of Violence*, *1*, 202–215. http://dx.doi.org/10.1037/a0023962

Noll, J. G., Trickett, P. K., & Putnam, F. W. (2003). A prospective investigation of the impact of childhood sexual abuse on the development of sexuality. *Journal of Consulting and Clinical Psychology*, *71*, 575–586.

Odgers, C. L., Moretti, M. M., & Reppucci, N. D. (2010). A review of findings from the "Gender and Aggression Project" informing juvenile justice policy and practice through gender-sensitive research. *Court Review*, *46*, 6–8.

Ogawa, J. R., Sroufe, L. A., Weinfield, N. S., Carlson, E. A., & Egeland, B. (1997). Development and the fragmented self: Longitudinal study of dissociative symptomatology in a nonclinical sample. *Development and Psychopathology*, *9*, 855–879. http://dx.doi.org/10.1017/S0954579497001478

Orcutt, H. K., Erickson, D. J., & Wolfe, J. (2002). A prospective analysis of trauma exposure: The mediating role of PTSD symptomatology. *Journal of Traumatic Stress*, *15*, 259–266. http://dx.doi.org/10.1023/A:1015215630493

Osofsky, J. D., & Lieberman, A. F. (2011). A call for integrating a mental health perspective into systems of care for abused and neglected infants and young children. *American Psychologist*, *66*, 120–128. http://dx.doi.org/10.1037/a0021630

Oudekerk, B. A., & Reppucci, N. D. (2009). Romantic relationships matter for girls' criminal trajectories: Recommendations for juvenile justice. *Court Review*, *46*, 52–57.

Overmeyer, S., Taylor, E., Blanz, B., & Schmidt, M. H. (1999). Psychosocial adversities underestimated in hyperkinetic children. *Journal of Child Psychology and Psychiatry*, *40*, 259–263. http://dx.doi.org/10.1111/1469-7610.00439

Patterson, G. R., Reid, J. B., & Dishion, T. J. (1992). *Antisocial boys* (Vol. 4). Eugene, OR: Castalia.

REFERENCES

Pears, K. C., & Fisher, P. A. (2005). Emotion understanding and theory of mind among maltreated children in foster care: Evidence of deficits. *Development and Psychopathology, 17*, 47–65. http://dx.doi.org/10.1017/S0954579405050030

Pears, K. C., Kim, H. K., Fisher, P. A., & Yoerger, K. (2013). Early school engagement and late elementary outcomes for maltreated children in foster care. *Developmental Psychology, 49*, 2201–2211. http://dx.doi.org/10.1037/a0032218

Pelzer, D. (1997). *The lost boy: A foster child's search for the love of a family.* Deerfield Beach, FL: Health Communications.

Pelzer, D. (2010). *A man named Dave.* London, England: Hachette.

Pelzer, D. (2014). *Too close to me: The middle-aged consequences of revealing a child called "It"* [Kindle ed.]. Retrieved from http://www.amazon.com/Too-Close-Middle-Aged-Consequences-Revealing-ebook/dp/B00L1HYMZU

Phillips, D. A., & Shonkoff, J. P. (Eds.). (2000). *From neurons to neighborhoods: The science of early childhood development.* Washington, DC: National Academy Press.

Pollak, S. D., Cicchetti, D., Hornung, K., & Reed, A. (2000). Recognizing emotion in faces: Developmental effects of child abuse and neglect. *Developmental Psychology, 36*, 679–688. http://dx.doi.org/10.1037/0012-1649.36.5.679

Pond, A., & Spinazzola, J. (2013). Editorial introduction: Residential services for children and adolescents impacted by family violence and trauma. *Journal of Family Violence, 28*, 635–638.

Putnam, F. W. (1997). *Dissociation in children and adolescents: A developmental perspective.* New York, NY: Guilford Press.

Putnam, F. W., Helmers, K., & Trickett, P. K. (1993). Development, reliability, and validity of a child dissociation scale. *Child Abuse & Neglect, 17*, 731–741. http://dx.doi.org/10.1016/S0145-2134(08)80004-X

Pynoos, R. S. (1993). Traumatic stress and developmental psychopathology in children and adolescents. *Review of Psychiatry, 12*, 205–238.

Raabe, F. J., & Spengler, D. (2013). Epigenetic risk factors in PTSD and depression. *Frontiers in Psychiatry, 4*, 80. http://dx.doi.org/10.3389/fpsyt.2013.00080

Racco, A., & Vis, J.-A. (2015). Evidence based trauma treatment for children and youth. *Child & Adolescent Social Work Journal, 32*, 121–129. http://dx.doi.org/10.1007/s10560-014-0347-3

Read, J., van Os, J., Morrison, A. P., & Ross, C. A. (2005). Childhood trauma, psychosis and schizophrenia: A literature review with theoretical and clinical implications. *Acta Psychiatrica Scandinavica, 112*, 330–350. http://dx.doi.org/10.1111/j.1600-0447.2005.00634.x

Rhodes, J. E., Haight, W. L., & Briggs, E. C. (1999). The influence of mentoring on the peer relationships of foster youth in relative and nonrelative care. *Journal of Research on Adolescence, 9*, 185–201.

Richards, L. M.-E. (2013). It is time for a more integrated bio-psycho-social approach to ADHD. *Clinical Child Psychology and Psychiatry, 18*, 483–503. http://dx.doi.org/10.1177/1359104512458228

Robertiello, G., & Terry, K. J. (2007). Can we profile sex offenders? A review of sex offender typologies. *Aggression and Violent Behavior, 12*, 508–518. http://dx.doi.org/10.1016/j.avb.2007.02.010

Rogosch, F. A., Cicchetti, D., Shields, A., & Toth, S. L. (1995). *Handbook of parenting: Vol. 4. Parenting dysfunction in child maltreatment* (pp. 127–159). Hillsdale, NJ: Erlbaum.

Rosenbluth, B. (2004). *Expect Respect: A support group curriculum for safe and healthy relationships.* Austin, TX: SafePlace.

Russell, B. S., Trudeau, J., & Britner, P. A. (2008). Intervention type matters in primary prevention of abusive head injury: Event history analysis results. *Child Abuse & Neglect, 32*, 949–957. http://dx.doi.org/10.1016/j.chiabu.2008.05.002

Ryan, C., & Siebens, J. (2012). *Educational attainment in the United States: 2009.* Retrieved from the U.S. Census Bureau: http://www.census.gov/prod/2012pubs/p20-566.pdf

Ryan, J. P., Williams, A. B., & Courtney, M. E. (2013). Adolescent neglect, juvenile delinquency and the risk of recidivism. *Journal of Youth and Adolescence, 42*, 454–465. http://dx.doi.org/10.1007/s10964-013-9906-8

Sales, J. M., Merrill, N. A., & Fivush, R. (2013). Does making meaning make it better? Narrative meaning making and well-being in at-risk African-American adolescent females. *Memory, 21*, 97–110. http://dx.doi.org/10.1080/09658211.2012.706614

Salzinger, S., Rosario, M., & Feldman, R. S. (2007). Physical child abuse and adolescent violent delinquency: The mediating and moderating roles of personal relationships. *Child Maltreatment, 33*, 208–219.

Sameroff, A. J., & Fiese, B. H. (2000). Transactional regulation: The developmental ecology of early intervention. *Handbook of early childhood intervention* (2nd ed., pp. 135–159). New York, NY: Cambridge University Press.

Sampson, R. (2002). *Acquaintance rape of college students* (Problem-Oriented Guides for Police Series, No. 17). Washington, DC: U.S. Department of Justice, Office of Community Oriented Policing Services. Retrieved from http://dx.doi.org/10.1037/e375052004-001

Sandberg, D. A., & Lynn, S. J. (1992). Dissociative experiences, psychopathology and adjustment, and child and adolescent maltreatment in female college students. *Journal of Abnormal Psychology, 101*, 717–723. http://dx.doi.org/10.1037/0021-843X.101.4.717

Sandberg, D. A., Lynn, S. J., & Matorin, A. I. (2001). Information processing of an acquaintance rape scenario among high- and low-dissociating college women. *Journal of Traumatic Stress, 14*, 585–603. http://dx.doi.org/10.1023/A:1011168808683

Saul, J., & Audage, N. C. (2007). *Preventing child sexual abuse within youth-serving organizations: Getting started on policies and procedures.* Atlanta, GA: Centers for Disease Control and Prevention.

Scannapieco, M., & Connell-Carrick, K. (2002). Focus on the first years: An eco-developmental assessment of child neglect for children 0 to 3 years of age. *Children and Youth Services Review, 24*, 601–621. http://dx.doi.org/10.1016/S0190-7409(02)00210-4

Scheeringa, M. S., Amaya-Jackson, L., & Cohen, J. (2002). *Preschool PTSD treatment manual.* Retrieved from http://www.infantinstitute.org/MikeSPDF/PPTversion7.pdf

Scheeringa, M. S., Zeanah, C. H., & Cohen, J. A. (2011). PTSD in children and adolescents: Toward an empirically based algorithm. *Depression and Anxiety, 28*, 770–782. http://dx.doi.org/10.1002/da.20736

Scheeringa, M. S., Zeanah, C. H., Drell, M. J., & Larrieu, J. A. (1995). Two approaches to the diagnosis of posttraumatic stress disorder in infancy and early childhood. *Journal of the American Academy of Child and Adolescent Psychiatry, 34*, 191–200. http://dx.doi.org/10.1097/00004583-199502000-00014

Schneider-Rosen, K., & Cicchetti, D. (1991). Early self-knowledge and emotional development: Visual self-recognition and affective reactions to mirror self-images in maltreated and non-maltreated toddlers. *Developmental Psychology, 27*, 471–478. http://dx.doi.org/10.1037/0012-1649.27.3.471

Schnitzer, P. G., & Ewigman, B. G. (2005). Child deaths resulting from inflicted injuries: Household risk factors and perpetrator characteristics. *Pediatrics, 116*, e687–e693. http://dx.doi.org/10.1542/peds.2005-0296

Schwartz, S. E., Rhodes, J. E., Chan, C. S., & Herrera, C. (2011). The impact of school-based mentoring on youths with different relational profiles. *Developmental Psychology, 47*, 450–462.

Schwimmer, D., Quivers, R., Mark McGwire Foundation for Children, Discovery Health Channel (Producers), Roth, V., & Dickson, A. (Directors). (2002). *Close to home.* United States: Direct Cinema Ltd.

Sedlak, A. (2010). *Fourth national incidence study of child abuse and neglect (NIS–4): Report to Congress.* Washington, DC: U.S. Department of Health and Human Services, Administration for Children and Families.

Settersten, R. A., Jr., & Ray, B. (2010). What's going on with young people today? The long and twisting path to adulthood. *The Future of Children, 20*, 19–41. http://dx.doi.org/10.1353/foc.0.0044

Shaw, D. S., Gilliom, M., Ingoldsby, E. M., & Nagin, D. S. (2003). Trajectories leading to school-age conduct problems. *Developmental Psychology, 39*, 189–200.

REFERENCES

Shonk, S. M., & Cicchetti, D. (2001). Maltreatment, competency deficits, and risk for academic and behavioral maladjustment. *Developmental Psychology, 37*, 3–17. http://dx.doi.org/10.1037/0012-1649.37.1.3

Sibert, J. R., Payne, E. H., Kemp, A. M., Barber, M., Rolfe, K., Morgan, R. J. H., . . . Butler, I. (2002). The incidence of severe physical child abuse in Wales. *Child Abuse & Neglect, 26*, 267–276. http://dx.doi.org/10.1016/S0145-2134(01)00324-6

Siegel, D. J. (2014). *Brainstorm: The power and purpose of the teenage brain.* New York, NY: Penguin.

Silberg, J. L. (1998). *The dissociative child: Diagnosis, treatment, and management.* Brooklandville, MD: Sidran Press.

Silberg, J. L. (2013). *The child survivor: Healing developmental trauma and dissociation.* New York, NY: Routledge.

Silverman, S. (1996). *Because I remember terror, father, I remember you.* Athens: University of Georgia Press.

Simon, V. A., Feiring, C., & McElroy, S. K. (2010). Making meaning of traumatic events: Youths' strategies for processing childhood sexual abuse are associated with psychosocial adjustment. *Child Maltreatment, 15*, 229–241.

Smith, C. A., Thornberry, T. P., & Ireland, T. O. (2004). Adolescent maltreatment and its impact: Timing matters. *The Prevention Researcher, 11*, 7–11.

Snyder, H. N. (2000, July). *Sexual assault of young children as reported to law enforcement: Victim, incident, and offender characteristics* [NIBRS Statistical Report]. Washington, DC: Bureau of Justice Statistics, Office of Justice Programs, U.S. Department of Justice. Retrieved from http://www.bjs.gov/content/pub/pdf/saycrle.pdf

Solomon, J. E., & George, C. E. (1999). *Attachment disorganization.* New York, NY: Guilford Press.

Southall, D. P., Plunkett, M. C., Banks, M. W., Falkov, A. F., & Samuels, M. P. (1997). Covert video recordings of life-threatening child abuse: Lessons for child protection. *Pediatrics, 100*, 735–760. http://dx.doi.org/10.1542/peds.100.5.735

Sroufe, L. A. (1986). Bowlby's contribution to psychoanalytic theory and developmental psychology; attachment: separation: loss. *Journal of Child Psychology and Psychiatry, and Allied Disciplines, 27*, 841–849. http://dx.doi.org/10.1111/j.1469-7610.1986.tb00203.x

Sroufe, L. A. (1990). An organizational perspective on the self. In D. Cicchetti & M. Beeghly (Eds.), *The self in transition: Infancy to childhood* (pp. 281–307). Chicago, IL: The University of Chicago Press.

Sroufe, L. A. (2009). The concept of development in developmental psychopathology. *Child Development Perspectives, 3*, 178–183. http://dx.doi.org/10.1111/j.1750-8606.2009.00103.x

Sroufe, L. A., Egeland, B., Carlson, E. A., & Collins, W. A. (2005). *The development of the person: The Minnesota study of risk and adaptation from birth to adulthood.* New York, NY: Guilford Press.

Starling, S. P., Patel, S., Burke, B. L., Sirotnak, A. P., Stronks, S., & Rosquist, P. (2004). Analysis of perpetrator admissions to inflicted traumatic brain injury in children. *Archives of Pediatrics & Adolescent Medicine, 158,* 454–458. http://dx.doi.org/10.1001/archpedi.158.5.454

Stewart, A., Livingston, M., & Dennison, S. (2008). Transitions and turning points: Examining the links between child maltreatment and juvenile offending. *Child Abuse & Neglect, 32,* 51–66. http://dx.doi.org/10.1016/j.chiabu.2007.04.011

Stormshak, E. A., Bierman, K. L., McMahon, R. J., & Lengua, L. J., & the Conduct Problems Prevention Research Group. (2000). Parenting practices and child disruptive behavior problems in early elementary school. *Journal of Clinical Child Psychology, 29,* 17–29. http://dx.doi.org/10.1207/S15374424jccp2901_3

Straus, M. A. (2000). Corporal punishment and primary prevention of physical abuse. *Child Abuse & Neglect, 24,* 1109–1114. http://dx.doi.org/10.1016/S0145-2134(00)00180-0

Straus, M. A. (2001). *Beating the devil out of them: Corporal punishment in American families and its effects on children.* Piscataway, NJ: Transaction.

Straus, M. A. (2005). Children should never, ever, be spanked no matter what the circumstances. In D. R. Loseke, R. J. Gelles, & M. M. Cavanaugh (Eds.), *Current controversies on family violence* (pp. 137–157). Thousand Oaks, CA: Sage.

Straus, M. A., & Field, C. J. (2003). Psychological aggression by American parents: National data on prevalence, chronicity, and severity. *Journal of Marriage and Family, 65,* 795–808. Retrieved from http://www.jstor.org/stable/3599891

Straus, M. A., & Stewart, J. H. (1999). Corporal punishment by American parents: National data on prevalence, chronicity, severity, and duration, in relation to child and family characteristics. *Clinical Child and Family Psychology Review, 2,* 55–70. http://dx.doi.org/10.1023/A:1021891529770

Stuewig, J., & McCloskey, L. A. (2005). The relation of child maltreatment to shame and guilt among adolescents: Psychological routes to depression and delinquency. *Child Maltreatment, 10,* 324–336. http://dx.doi.org/10.1177/1077559505279308

Swannell, S., Martin, G., Page, A., Hasking, P., Hazell, P., Taylor, A., & Protani, M. (2012). Child maltreatment, subsequent non-suicidal self-injury and the mediating roles of dissociation, alexithymia and self-blame. *Child Abuse & Neglect, 36,* 572–584.

Taylor, M. (1999). *Imaginary companions and the children who create them.* New York, NY: Oxford University Press.

REFERENCES

Teicher, M. H. (2000). Wounds that time won't heal: The neurobiology of child abuse. *Cerebrum*, 2, 50–67.

TF-CBT Web. (2005). *TF-CBT Web. A web-based learning course for trauma-focused cognitive-behavioral therapy.* Retrieved from http://tfcbt.musc.edu

Thompson, R. A. (2000). The legacy of early attachments. *Child Development*, 71, 145–152. http://dx.doi.org/10.1111/1467-8624.00128

Tomasello, M. (1995). Joint attention as social cognition. In C. Moore & P. J. Dunham (Eds.), *Joint attention: Its origins and role in development* (pp. 103–130). Hillsdale, NJ: Lawrence Erlbaum Associates.

Toth, S. L., & Cicchetti, D. (2013). A developmental psychopathology perspective on child maltreatment. Introduction. *Child Maltreatment*, 18, 135–139. http://dx.doi.org/10.1177/1077559513500380

Toth, S. L., Cicchetti, D., Macfie, J., & Emde, R. N. (1997). Representations of self and other in the narratives of neglected, physically abused, and sexually abused preschoolers. *Development and Psychopathology*, 9, 781–796. http://dx.doi.org/10.1017/S0954579497001430

Toth, S. L., Maughan, A., Manly, J. T., Spagnola, M., & Cicchetti, D. (2002). The relative efficacy of two interventions in altering maltreated preschool children's representational models: Implications for attachment theory. *Development and Psychopathology*, 14, 877–908. http://dx.doi.org/10.1017/S095457940200411X

Trauma and Learning Policy Initiative. (n.d.). *Helping traumatized children learn.* Retrieved from http://traumasensitiveschools.org

Trickett, P. K., & Gordis, E. B. (2004). Aggression and antisocial behavior in sexually abused females. In M. Putallaz & K. L. Bierman (Eds.), *Aggression, antisocial behavior, and violence among girls* (pp. 162–185). New York, NY: Guilford Press.

Trickett, P. K., & McBride-Chang, C. (1995). The developmental impact of different forms of child abuse and neglect. *Developmental Review*, 15, 311–337. http://dx.doi.org/10.1006/drev.1995.1012

Trickett, P. K., Negriff, S., Ji, J., & Peckins, M. (2011). Child maltreatment and adolescent development. *Journal of Research on Adolescence*, 21, 3–20.

Trickett, P. K., Noll, J. G., & Putnam, F. W. (2011). The impact of sexual abuse on female development: Lessons from a multigenerational, longitudinal research study. *Development and Psychopathology*, 23, 453–476.

Trickett, P. K., & Putnam, F. W. (1993). Impact of child sexual abuse on females: Toward a developmental, psychobiological integration. *Psychological Science*, 4, 81–87. http://dx.doi.org/10.1111/j.1467-9280.1993.tb00465.x

Tulloch, M. (2000). The meaning of age differences in the fear of crime. *British Journal of Criminology*, 40, 451–467. http://dx.doi.org/10.1093/bjc/40.3.451

REFERENCES

Turner, P. K., Runtz, M. G., & Galambos, N. L. (1999). Sexual abuse, pubertal timing, and subjective age in adolescent girls: A research note. *Journal of Reproductive and Infant Psychology, 17*, 111–118. http://dx.doi.org/10.1080/02646839908409091

U.S. Attorney's Office. (2011, May 26). *Former Cal State East Bay professor pleads guilty to aggravated sexual abuse of a child.* Retrieved from https://www.fbi.gov/sanfrancisco/press-releases/2011/sf052611a.htm

U.S. Department of Education. (2004). *Educator sexual misconduct: A synthesis of existing literature.* Washington, DC: Author.

U.S. Department of Health and Human Services, Administration for Children and Families. (2010). *Child abuse and neglect statistics.* Washington, DC: Author. Retrieved from http://childwelfare.gov/systemwide/statistics/can.cfm

U.S. Department of Health and Human Services, Administration for Children and Families, Administration on Children, Youth and Families, Children's Bureau. (2012). *Child maltreatment 2012.* Retrieved from http://www.acf.hhs.gov/sites/default/files/cb/cm2012.pdf#page=31

Valentino, K., Cicchetti, D., Toth, S. L., & Rogosch, F. A. (2006). Mother–child play and emerging social behaviors among infants from maltreating families. *Developmental Psychology, 42*, 474–485.

Vanderwert, R. E., Marshall, P. J., Nelson, C. A., III, Zeanah, C. H., & Fox, N. A. (2010). Timing of intervention affects brain electrical activity in children exposed to severe psychosocial neglect. *PLoS ONE, 5*, e11415. http://dx.doi.org/10.1371/journal.pone.0011415

Veltman, M. W. M., & Browne, K. D. (2001). Three decades of child maltreatment research: Implications for the school years. *Trauma, Violence, and Abuse: A Review Journal, 2*, 215–239.

Walsh, K., Galea, S., & Koenen, K. C. (2012). Mechanisms underlying sexual violence exposure and psychosocial sequelae: A theoretical and empirical review. *Clinical Psychology: Science and Practice, 19*, 260–275. http://dx.doi.org/10.1111/cpsp.12004

Washington State University Extension. (n.d.). *Complex trauma.* Retrieved from http://ext100.wsu.edu/cafru/complex-trauma-2/

Weinstein, D., Staffelbach, D., & Biaggio, M. (2000). Attention-deficit hyperactivity disorder and posttraumatic stress disorder: Differential diagnosis in childhood sexual abuse. *Clinical Psychology Review, 20*, 359–378. http://dx.doi.org/10.1016/S0272-7358(98)00107-X

Weller, J. A., Leve, L. D., Kim, H. K., Bhimji, J., & Fisher, P. A. (2015). Plasticity of risky decision making among maltreated adolescents: Evidence from a randomized controlled trial. *Development and Psychopathology, 27*(Special Issue 2), 535–551. http://dx.doi.org/10.1017/S0954579415000140

Wellman, H. M. (2002). Understanding the psychological world: Developing a theory of mind. *Blackwell handbook of childhood cognitive development* (pp. 167–187). Malden, MA: Blackwell.

Widom, C. S. (2003). Understanding child maltreatment and juvenile delinquency: The research. In J. Wiig, C. S. Widom, & J. A. Tuell (Eds.), *Understanding child maltreatment and juvenile delinquency: From research to effective program, practice, and systematic solutions* (pp. 1–10). Washington, DC: CWLA Press.

Widom, C. S., Schuck, A. M., & White, H. R. (2006). An examination of pathways from childhood victimization to violence: The role of early aggression and problematic alcohol use. *Violence and Victims, 21*, 675–690.

Widom, C. S., & White, H. R. (1997). Problem behaviours in abused and neglected children grown up: Prevalence and co-occurrence of substance abuse, crime and violence. *Criminal Behaviour and Mental Health, 7*, 287–310.

Wolfe, D. A., Crooks, C. C., Chiodo, D., & Jaffe, P. (2009). Child maltreatment, bullying, gender-based harassment, and adolescent dating violence: Making the connections. *Psychology of Women Quarterly, 33*, 21–24. http://dx.doi.org/10.1111/j.1471-6402.2008.01469.x

Wolfe, D. A., Wekerle, C., Reitzel-Jaffe, D., Grasley, C., Pittman, A. L., & MacEachran, A. (1997). Interrupting the cycle of violence: Empowering youth to promote healthy relationships. In D. A. Wolfe, R. J. McMahon, & R. D. Peters (Eds.), *Child abuse: New directions in prevention and treatment across the life span* (pp. 102–129). Thousand Oaks, CA: Sage.

Wolff, P. H. (1987). *The development of behavioral states and the expression of emotions in early infancy: New proposals for investigation.* Chicago, IL: University of Chicago Press.

World Health Organization. (2010). *World report on violence and health.* Geneva, Switzerland: Author.

Zabin, L. S., Emerson, M. R., & Rowland, D. L. (2005). Childhood sexual abuse and early menarche: The direction of their relationship and its implications. *Journal of Adolescent Health, 36*, 393–400. http://dx.doi.org/10.1016/j.jadohealth.2004.07.013

Zeanah, C. H., Fox, N. A., & Nelson, C. A. (2012). The Bucharest Early Intervention Project: Case study in the ethics of mental health research. *Journal of Nervous and Mental Disease, 200*, 243–247. http://dx.doi.org/10.1097/NMD.0b013e318247d275

Zurbriggen, E. L., & Freyd, J. J. (2004). The link between child sexual abuse and risky sexual behavior: The role of dissociative tendencies, information-processing effects, and consensual sex decision mechanisms. In J. Koenig, L. S. Doll, A. O'Leary, and W. Pequegnat (Eds.), *From child sexual abuse to adult sexual risk: Trauma, revictimization, and intervention* (pp. 135–157). Washington, DC: American Psychological Association.

Index

Abuse. *See specific types*
Academic maladjustment, 64–65
Academic success, 64–65
Accidental falls, in infancy, 24
Acts of commission, 77
Acts of omission, 77
Adaptation, 13, 14
ADHD (attention-deficit/hyperactivity disorder), 62–64
Adjustment, 64–65, 73–74
Administer Researcher Campus Climate Consortium, 104
Adolescence, 73–89. *See also* Early adolescence; Late adolescence
    developmental implications of maltreatment in, 80–85, 112–115
    developmental pathways in, 75–76
    disruptions to developmental processes in, 109–111
    and emerging adulthood, 93
    externalizing behaviors in, 40
    interventions for maltreated adolescents, 85–87, 115
    maltreatment in childhood vs., 73–75
    misconceptions about maltreatment in, 88
    neglect in, 76–77
    normative development in, 106–108
    physical abuse in, 80
    posttraumatic stress and dissociation in, 87–88
    preventing maltreatment in, 86
    psychological abuse in, 79–80
    resources on maltreatment in, 88–89
    sexual abuse in, 77–79
    sexual offending in, 40
    sources of resilience in, 75
    vulnerability of girls in, 104
Adolescent Dissociative Experiences Scale, 87–88
Adolescent onset maltreatment, 75–76
Adulthood, emerging. *See* Emerging adulthood
AF-CBT (Alternatives for Families CBT), 68
Affect, 43, 65
Agency, of adolescents, 74–75
Aggression, 58–59, 78, 82
Aggressiveness, 79
Alcohol use disorder, 99, 100
Alternatives for Families CBT (AF-CBT), 68

INDEX

Amaya-Jackson, L., 51
American Academy of Pediatrics, 26, 40, 42
American Camping Association, 7
Anger, physical abuse and, 24, 38–39
Ansell-Casey Life Skills Assessment, 94
Antisocial behaviors, 74, 76, 82–85
Arnett, Jeffrey Jensen, 92
Arousal, 13, 49, 84
Attachment
  disruptions in, 109
  and maltreatment in infancy/toddlerhood, 30
  and maltreatment in preschool-age childhood, 42–43
  and mentoring adolescents, 87
  normative, 107
  and resilience, 29–30
  between siblings, 66–67
Attention-deficit/hyperactivity disorder (ADHD), 62–64
Attention dysregulation, 62–64
Autism, 44
Avery, R. J., 95
Avoidance, 49

Banks, M. W., 23
Baylin, J., 35
Because I Remember Terror, Father, I Remember You (Silverman), 89
Behavior(s)
  antisocial, 74, 76, 82–85
  challenging, 69–70, 88
  determinants of, 29
  externalizing, 40, 80
  risky, 78, 81
  self-harming, 78
  sexual, by preschoolers, 40–42, 52
  zero-tolerance policies for, 70–71
Behavioral engagement, 65
Behavioral problems
  in middle childhood, 68
  in preschoolers, 37
  in toddlerhood, 27

Behavioral Tech, 102
Behavior management, 69–70
Berlin, L. J., 46, 47
Biological sensitivity to context, 15
Birth parents, attachment to, 30
Blair, C., 16
Blanz, B., 63–64
Blaustein, M. E., 89
Boden, J. M., 99
Bowlby, J., 42
Boynton-Jarrett, R., 60
Boys
  challenging behaviors of, 88
  dating violence prevention programs for, 86
  physical abuse of, 80, 88
  sexual abuse of, 57, 78
Bradshaw, John, 10
Brain-Based Parenting (Hughes & Baylin), 35
Brain development, in adolescence, 75
Brain injuries, 23–25
Brainstorm: The Power and Purpose of the Teenage Brain (Siegel), 89
Breen, J., 21–22
Brief interruptions in care, for infants, 27–28
Brookes, R. B., 17
Browne, K., 57
Bruce, J., 45
Bucharest Early Intervention Project, 28–29, 31, 45

A Call to Action on Behalf of Maltreated Infants and Toddlers (Cohen, Cole, & Jaclyn), 35
Camps, prevention programs for, 7
Campus climate survey, 104
Care
  brief interruptions in, 27–28
  family-based, 31–32
  institutionalized, 28–29. *See also* Orphanages

INDEX

Caregivers. *See also* Parents
  attachment with, 30, 42–43
  development of narratives with, 46–48
  of preschool-age children, 37, 42–48
  of school-age children, 56
  and theory of mind development, 44–46
Casey Life Skills, 102
Cassidy, J., 46, 47
CBT. *See* Cognitive behavioral therapy
Center on the Developing Child, 17, 34–35
Challenging behaviors, 69–70, 88
Chang, L., 80
Child Dissociative Checklist, 50
Child maltreatment
  current research on, 103–104
  definitions of, 3–4
  maltreatment in adolescence vs., 73–75
Child–Parent Psychotherapy (CPP), 51, 53
Child protective workers, 21–22
Children's Bureau, 65
Child Sexual Behavior Inventory, 42
The Child Survivor (Silberg), 50, 54, 72, 87
Chisholm, J. S., 60–61
Churches, prevention programs for, 7
Cicchetti, D., 43, 45, 64
Close to Home (film), 72
Cognition(s)
  PTSD and, 49
  social, 43–45
  trauma-specific, 68
Cognitive behavioral therapy (CBT)
  with adolescents, 85
  with preschool-age children, 51, 53
  with school-age children, 68
  trauma-focused, 51, 53, 68, 85
Cognitive development, 106, 109

Cognitive engagement, 65
Cognitive processing therapy, 85
Cohen, J., 35, 89
Cole, P., 31, 35
Cole, S. F., 71
College, transitioning to, 95–96, 104
Commission, acts of, 77
Commitment statements, 32
Community, effect of maltreatment on, 7–8
Confidence, 57
Conflict
  parent–child, 75–76
  sibling, 65–66
Confrontation, avoiding, 45
Corporal punishment, 38–39
Costs, of child maltreatment, 6
CPP (Child–Parent Psychotherapy), 51, 53
Crossover youth, 75
Crying, as trigger for abuse, 24, 25, 32

Dating, 79, 86
Davis, J. L., 96
Death, maltreatment-related, 20, 25, 32
Deblinger, E., 89
Delinquency
  among adolescents, 74, 78, 82–84
  and emotion regulation, 83
  and friendship, 78
  and school disengagement, 83
  and sexual abuse, 82
  and timing of puberty, 61
Depression, 61
The Developing Mind (Siegel), 17
Development
  cognitive, 106, 109
  as context for maltreatment, 5
  determinants of, 29
  emotional, 107, 110
  family, 108
  language, 31, 106
  memory, 107, 111

INDEX

Development (*continued*)
   moral, 108, 110
   normative, 5, 30–31, 50
   self, 107, 110
   sexual, 41–42
   social, 13, 108, 111
Developmental needs, of school-age children, 56
Developmental pathways, 61, 75–76
Developmental processes
   and developmental psychopathology perspective, 9–11
   and maltreatment in adolescence, 80–85
   and maltreatment in infancy, 27–30
   and maltreatment in preschool-age childhood, 41–50
   and maltreatment in toddlerhood, 27–31
   maltreatment/violence exposure and disruptions to, 109–111
   normative, 106–108
   as targets for interventions, 112–115
Developmental psychopathology, 3–17
   developmental context in, 5
   and developmental trajectories, 11–13
   ecological context in, 6–9
   emerging adulthood in, 91–92
   emerging perspectives on, 13–16
   maladaptation and adaptation in, 13, 14
   processes in, 9–11
   resources on, 17
   studies of resilience in, 29
   and vulnerability of late-adolescent girls and emerging adult women, 104
Developmental trajectories, 11–13, 31, 76

Developmental traumatology, 4
Developmental victimology, 4
"Development and Feasibility of a Sibling Intervention for Youth in Foster Care" (Kothari et al.), 72
Diabetes, 6
Diagnostic and Statistical Manual of Mental Disorders, Fourth Edition, 99
Diagnostic and Statistical Manual of Mental Disorders, Fifth Edition (DSM–5), 49
Diagnostic Infant and Preschool Assessment (DIPA), 35
Differential susceptibility, 15
Discrete behavioral state theory, 62
Disorganized attachment, 43
Dissociation
   in adolescence, 84, 87–88
   in emerging adults, 95–97
   and emotion regulation, 84
   and posttraumatic stress, 87–88
   in preschool-age childhood, 49–50
   in school-age children, 61–62, 70
   and self-regulation, 61–62
   and sexual intimacy issues, 96–97
   and transition to college, 95
   and traumatic stress, 49–50
Dissociation in Children and Adolescents (Putnam), 50, 87, 88
The Dissociative Child (Silberg), 50, 87
Dissociative disorders, 49–50
Distress, of preschool-age children, 49
Dodge, K. A., 80
Domestic violence, 41. *See also* Intimate partner violence
DSM–5 (Diagnostic and Statistical Manual of Mental Disorders, Fifth Edition), 49
Dysphoric arousal, 84

INDEX

Early adolescence
   disruptions to developmental
      processes in, 109–111
   impact of maltreatment/exposure
      to violence in, 112–115
   intervention targets for
      maltreatment in, 115
   normative development in,
      106–108
Eating disorders, 61
Ecological context for maltreatment,
   6–9
Elliott, M., 57
Emde, R. N., 43
Emerging adulthood, 91–102
   disruptions to developmental
      processes in, 109–111
   effects of child maltreatment in, 9,
      112–115
   features of, 91–94
   interventions for emerging adults,
      100–101, 115
   misconceptions about, 101
   normative development in,
      106–108
   resources on, 102
   sexual intimacy issues in, 96–98
   substance abuse challenges in,
      98–100
   transition from foster care to
      independence in, 94–95
   transition to college in, 95–96
   vulnerability of women in, 104
Emotional abuse, 99
Emotional development, 107, 110
Emotional intimacy, 96
Emotional numbing, 84
Emotional problems, in preschool-age
   children, 37
Emotional reactions, of toddlers, 31
Emotional regulation
   by adolescents, 79, 83–84
   by school-age children, 70

Empathic understanding, 97–98
Empathy, 44
Engagement
   behavioral, 65
   cognitive, 65
   school, 64–65, 84–85
Environment, interactions of genetics
   and, 13–16, 101
Epigenetics, 14–15, 98
Equifinality, 12, 44, 64
Events, narratives about, 46–48
Evidence-based trauma-focused
   mental health care, 3
Evolutionary theory, 60
Exclusion, behavior management
   by, 69
Expectations, parental, 38–39
Expect Respect, 86
Experiential canonization model,
   15–16
The Explosive Child (Greene), 71
Externalizing behaviors, 40, 80

Failure to launch, 101
Falkov, A. F., 23
False self, 43
Families, effect of maltreatment on,
   8–9, 111
Family-based care, 31–32
Family development, 108
Family members, abuse perpetrated
   by, 9, 57, 60, 79
Fathers, shaken baby syndrome
   prevention for, 32
Fear
   and dissociation, 62
   of sexual abuse, 58
   of sexuality and intimacy, 96
Feiring, C., 84
Fergusson, D. M., 99
Field, C. J., 58
Financial support, for emerging
   adults, 93–96

INDEX

Finkelhor, D., 77, 103
Fisher, P. A., 45, 65
Fivush, R., 46–48
Foster care
    attachment of children in, 30
    development of narratives with children in, 47
    for infants and toddlers, 31–32
    institutionalized care vs., 28–29
    placement of siblings in, 65–67, 71
    for preschool-age children, 51–52
    school engagement of children in, 65
    theory of mind abilities of children in, 45
    therapeutic, 51
    transition to independence from, 86, 94–95, 100
    treatment, 51
Foster Care Independence Act (1999), 94
FosterClub, 102
Fractures, abuse-related, 23, 24
Freundlich, M., 95
Freyd, J. J., 96–97
Friendship, 82

Gene–environment interactions, 13–16, 101
Gilbert, D., 4
Girls
    in antisocial peer groups, 82
    behavior management with, 70
    in dating violence prevention programs, 86
    delinquency of, 83
    physical abuse of, 80, 88
    school disengagement for, 84–85
    sexual maltreatment of, 26, 57–61, 70, 78, 79, 81, 84–85
    substance abuse by, 83–84
    timing of puberty in, 59–61
    vulnerability of, 104

Goldstein, A. L., 99, 100
Goldstein, S., 17
Good Things Too (film), 88
Grandparents, 9
Greene, R. W., 71
Gregg, C. R., 7

Hamby, S. L., 77
Handbook of Developmental Psychopathology (Lewis & Rudolph), 17
Handbook of Infant Mental Health (Zeanah), 35
Handbook of Resilience in Children (Goldstein & Brookes), 17
Hansen-Stamp, C., 7
Hartzwell, M., 17
Harvard University, 17, 34–35
Hazards, failure to protect from, 20
Helping Traumatized Children Learn (Cole et al.), 71
Hindle, D., 67
Horwood, L. J., 99
Hospital-based educational interventions, 32–33
Hughes, D. A., 35
Huth-Bocks, A. C., 41
Hyperkinetic disorder, 63–64

ICD. *See International Classification of Diseases, 10th Revision*
Identity exploration, 92, 93
Imaginary Friends Questionnaire, 50
Impulsivity problems, 63–64
"In between" feelings, 91–92
Incorrigible teenagers, 83
Independence, 86, 94–95, 100
Independent living programs, 94–95
Infancy, 19–35
    developmental effects of maltreatment in, 27–30, 112–115
    disruptions to developmental processes in, 109–111

interventions for maltreated
  infants, 30–31, 115
misconceptions about
  maltreatment in, 33–34
neglect in, 20–22, 28–30, 33, 62
normative development in,
  106–108
physical abuse in, 22–26, 32–33, 39
psychological abuse in, 26–27
resources on maltreatment in,
  34–35
sexual abuse in, 26, 31
Insecure attachment, 42–43, 61
Instability, age of, 92
Institute of Infant and Early
  Childhood Mental Health, 54
Institutionalized care, 28–29. *See also*
  Orphanages
Interdependence, 10
Interdependent living, 95
Intergenerational transmission,
  38, 101
Internalizing problems, 79
*International Classification of Diseases,
  10th Revision (ICD)*, 49, 50,
  63–64
International Society for the Study of
  Trauma and Dissociation, 50
Interpersonal relationships
  in adolescence, 80–82
  of adult survivors of maltreatment,
    9, 101
  of emerging adults, 93, 96–98, 100
  with mentors, 86–87
  between siblings, 67
Interruptions in care, for infants, 27–28
Interventions
  for alcohol use disorder, 100
  developmental processes as targets
    for, 115
  for emerging adults, 100–101
  for maltreated adolescents, 85–87
  for maltreated preschoolers, 51, 53

for maltreated school-age children,
  68–70
for neglected infants and toddlers,
  30–31
Intimacy, 96–98
Intimate partner violence, 79, 101. *See
  also* Domestic violence
Intrusion, 49
Ireland, T. O., 74
Isolation, 27–28
Iwaniec, D., 27

Jaclyn, S., 35
Ji, J., 76
Jones, L. M., 103
Journal of Family Violence, 85
Juvenile justice system, 75, 82–83,
  85, 88
Juveniles, sexual abuse perpetrated
  by, 40
Juvenile Victimization Questionnaire,
  104

Kerig, P. K., 80–81
Kidnappings, 7
Kilcoyne, J., 57
Kim, H. K., 65
Kinniburgh, K. M., 89
Koplow, L., 53
Kothari, B. H., 72

Language development, 31, 106
Lansford, J. E., 87
Late adolescence
  disruptions to developmental
    processes in, 109–111
  impact of maltreatment/exposure
    to violence in, 112–115
  intervention targets for
    maltreatment in, 115
  normative development in,
    106–108
  vulnerability of girls in, 104

INDEX

Lead exposure, 63
Leve, L. D., 54
Levendosky, A. A., 41
Lewis, M., 17
Limit-setting, 70–71
Linehan, Marsha, 102
A Little Problem at Home (film), 89
Loneliness, 27–28
Los Angeles, California, 75
The Lost Boy (Pelzer), 89
Lynn, S. J., 95, 97

Macfie, J., 43
Maladaptation, 13, 14
Maladjustment, academic, 64–65
Maltreatment
   in adolescence vs. childhood, 73–75
   by adult survivors of maltreatment, 101
   current research on, 103–104
   developmental context for, 5
   developmental psychopathology perspective on, 3–17
   disruptions to developmental processes from, 109–111
   ecological context for, 6–9
   effects of, in middle childhood, 59–67
Maltz, Wendy, 98, 102
Mandated reporters of abuse, 55
Manipulation, in sexual abuse, 57–58
Mannarino, A. P., 89
MAOA genotypes, 14
Marshall, N. A., 59
Massachusetts, trauma-sensitive schools in, 68
Masturbation, 52
Matorin, A. I., 97
Maturity, 88
Maughan, A., 45
McBride-Chang, C., 80
Meaning-making conversations, 48

Media portrayals, of survivors, 9–10
Medicaid, 94
Medical evaluations, of sexual abuse, 26
Medical neglect, 20
Memory
   of preschoolers, 46–48
   of toddlers and infants, 33
   for trauma, 111
Memory development, 107, 111
Mennuti-Washburn, J., 46, 47
Menstruation, timing of, 59–61
Mental health disorders, 61, 77
Mental health professionals, 63–67
Mentoring, 86–87
Merrill, N. A., 48
Middle childhood, 55–72. *See also* School-age childhood
   effects of maltreatment in, 59–67
   interventions for maltreated school-age children, 68–70
   misconceptions about maltreatment in, 70–71
   neglect in, 56
   physical abuse in, 56
   psychological abuse in, 58–59
   resources on maltreatment in, 71–72
   sexual abuse in, 57–58
Millwood, M., 97
Mind, theory of, 44–45
Minnesota Mother–Child project, 77
Mood, 49, 53
Moral development, 108, 110
Motivation, in behavior management, 69–70
Multidimensional Treatment Foster Care for Preschoolers aged 3 to 6 (MTFC-P), 51–52
Multifinality, 11–12, 32, 45
Myers, K., 21–22

Najavits, L. M., 102
Narratives, development of, 46–48

INDEX

National Child Traumatic Stress Network, 17
Naylor, R., 21–22
Needs
  neglect and difficulty meeting, 20
  of school-age children, 56
Negative representations, 43
Neglect, 5
  in adolescence, 76–77, 88
  in infancy, 20–22, 28–30, 33, 62
  in middle childhood, 56
  in preschool-age childhood, 38
  rates of, 3, 103
  self-serving narratives about, 47–48
  and substance abuse, 99
  in toddlerhood, 20–22, 33
Negriff, S., 76
Nondirective play therapy, 53
Normative development, 5, 30–31, 50

Omission, acts of, 77
Open-ended pretend play, 45, 53
Opportunistic pattern, of sexual offending, 39
Ormrod, R., 77
Orphanages
  need for human contact in, 26
  outcomes for children raised in, 28–29
  theory of mind development in, 45
Osofsky, J. D., 35
Overmeyer, S., 63–64

Parent–child conflicts, in adolescence, 75–76
Parenting from the Inside Out (Siegel & Hartzell), 17
Parents. *See also* Caregivers
  attachment to, 30
  expectations of, 38–39
  older siblings acting as, 66–67
  self-serving narratives of, 47–48
Pears, K. C., 45, 65

Peckins, M., 76
Peer relationships, in adolescence, 80–82
Pelzer, Dave, 10–11, 89
Petretic-Jackson, P. A., 96
Physical abuse
  in adolescence, 80, 87, 88
  and dissociation, 95
  in infancy, 22–26, 32–33, 39
  in middle childhood, 56
  posttraumatic stress associated with, 87
  in preschool-age childhood, 38–39, 47
  rates of, 103
  self-serving narratives about, 47
  and substance dependence, 99
  and timing of puberty, 60
  in toddlerhood, 22–23, 33
Physical examinations, for sexual abuse, 40, 53
Play therapy, 53
Plunkett, M. C., 23
Poisoning, 23
Polyvictimization, 76
Positive affect, false, 43
Posttraumatic stress
  adolescents with, 84, 85, 87–88
  and domestic violence, 41
  and emotion regulation, 84
  preschoolers with, 41
Posttraumatic stress disorder (PTSD), 15, 49, 63, 113
Poverty, stress response and, 16
"Practitioner Review: Children in Foster Care—Vulnerabilities and Evidence-Based Interventions that Promote Resilience Processes" (Leve et al.), 54
Preschool-age childhood, 37–54
  developmental effects of maltreatment in, 41–50, 112–115

Preschool-age childhood (*continued*)
  disruptions to developmental processes in, 109–111
  interventions for maltreated preschoolers, 51, 115
  misconceptions about maltreatment in, 52–53
  neglect in, 38
  normative development in, 106–108
  physical abuse in, 38–39, 56
  posttraumatic stress in, 87
  preventing maltreatment in, 51–52
  psychological abuse in, 40–41
  resources on maltreatment in, 53–54
  sexual abuse in, 39–40
Pretend play, 45, 50
Prevention of maltreatment, 3, 104
  in adolescence, 86
  in communities, 7–8
  in infancy, 32–33, 38–39
  in preschool-age childhood, 39, 51–52
Psychological abuse
  in adolescence, 79–80
  co-occurrence of, 80
  and dissociation, 95
  in infancy, 26–27
  in middle childhood, 58–59
  in preschool-age childhood, 40–41
  in toddlerhood, 26–27
Psychotherapy, with preschool-age children, 51, 53
PTSD. *See* Posttraumatic stress disorder
Puberty, 59–61
Punishment, 38–39, 48
Putnam, F. W., 31, 50, 61–62, 87, 88

Questions asked by caregivers, 46–48

Rage, 24
Raver, C. C., 16
Reactivity, 49
Reality testing, 97
Recovery, 10–11, 34
Resilience
  of adolescents, 74, 75
  of child maltreatment survivors, 9–11
  of children vs. adolescents, 74
  of children with coherent life narratives, 48
  in interpersonal relationships, 97–98
  of preschoolers, 48
  of toddlers and infants, 28–30, 34
  and trauma, 4
Revictimization, 81, 83, 87
Risk
  detection of, 97, 98
  differential susceptibility to, 15
Risk-taking, 73, 93
Risky behavior, 78, 81
Rogosch, F. A., 45
Romanian orphanages, 28–29, 31, 45
Romantic relationships, 81
Rudolph, K. D., 17
Ryan, J. P., 74

Safe Babies Court Teams, 35
Safe Dates, 86
Saito, K., 103
Sales, J. M., 46–48
Samuels, M. P., 23
Sandberg, D. A., 95, 97
Scheeringa, M. S., 51
Schmidt, M. H., 63–64
School(s)
  as protective factor, 55
  sexual abuse at, 58
  sexual abuse prevention programs in, 7–8
  trauma-sensitive, 3, 68–69

INDEX

School-age childhood. *See also* Middle childhood
   disruptions to developmental processes in, 109–111
   impact of maltreatment/exposure to violence in, 112–115
   intervention targets for maltreatment in, 115
   normative development in, 106–108
School engagement, 64–65, 84–85
Schwartz, D., 80
The Science of Neglect (Center on the Developing Child), 34–35
Secondary sex characteristics, 59–61
Secure attachment, 42
Seeking Safety (Najavits), 102
Self development, 107, 110
Self-esteem, 57
Self-focused age, 92
Self-harming behavior, 78
Self-medication model, 98
Self-regulation, 61–62
Self-serving narratives, of parents, 47–48
Semel, M. A., 41
Sense of self, 30–31
Separation of siblings, in foster care, 67
Sexual abuse
   in adolescence, 77–79
   as cause of sexual offending, 12, 13
   in infancy, 26, 31
   interventions following, 85
   in middle childhood, 57–58
   in preschool-age childhood, 39–40, 53
   rate of, 103
   school-based prevention programs, 7–8
   self-serving narratives about, 47
   sexual intimacy issues for survivors of, 96–98
   shame about, 84–85
   and substance dependence, 99
   in toddlerhood, 26, 31
Sexual activity, 60
Sexual behavior, by preschoolers, 40–42, 52
Sexual development, 41–42
Sexual Healing Journey (Maltz), 102
Sexual intimacy, 96–98
Sexuality, 81, 96
Sexual offenders
   access to school-age children for, 57–58
   childhood sexual abuse of, 12, 13
   diversity of, 39–40
   family vs. non–family, 57, 79
   targeting of preschoolers by, 39
   timing of puberty and relationship with, 60
Sexual victimization
   of adolescents, 77–78, 81
   of adult survivors of abuse, 97
Shaken baby syndrome, 24–26, 32–33
Shame, 84–85
Shapiro, D. L., 41
Shattuck, A., 103
Shonk, S. M., 64
Siblings
   foster care placement of, 65–67, 71
   unexpected deaths of, 23
Siegel, D., 17, 89
Silberg, J. L., 50, 54, 62, 72, 87
Silencing of narratives, 48
Silverman, S., 89
Sleeper effects of maltreatment, 81
Smith, C. A., 74
Social cognition, 43–45
Social development, 13, 108, 111
Social isolation, 27–28
Social relationships
   of preschoolers, 42–48
   and resilience of maltreated infants and toddlers, 30, 34
   of school-age children, 55

INDEX

Society, effect of maltreatment on, 6–8
Southall, D. P., 23
Spanking, 38–39
Special needs, foster care for children with, 66
Special relationships, of sex offenders and victims, 57–58
Sroufe, Alan, 29
Stewart, A., 74
Straus, M. A., 38, 58
Stress. *See also* Posttraumatic stress
    on adolescents, 74
    effects on infants and toddlers of, 27–29, 34
    and lack of care, 27–29
    and timing of puberty, 60–61
    traumatic, 49–50
Stress response, poverty and, 16
Stroke, 6
Structure, for school-age children, 70–71
Substance abuse, 22, 83–84, 98–101
Success, academic, 64–65
Suffocation, 23
Suicidal ideation, 78
Supervision, of children, 5
Support
    for emerging adults, 93–96
    between siblings, 66–67
Survival crimes, 83
Survivors of maltreatment
    developmental trajectories of, 11–13
    media portrayals of, 9–10
    recovery for, 10–11
    resilience of, 9–11
    sexual intimacy issues for, 96–98
    transition to college for, 95–96

TARGET *(Trauma Affect Regulation: Guide for Education and Therapy)*, 85
Taylor, E., 63–64

Teicher, M. H., 4
TF-CBT. *See* Trauma-focused CBT
TF-CBT Web, 72
Theory of mind, 44–45
Thornberry, T. P., 74
Toddlerhood, 19–35
    attachment in, 42
    developmental effects of maltreatment in, 27–31, 112–115
    disruptions to developmental processes in, 109–111
    interventions for neglected toddlers, 30–31, 115
    misconceptions about maltreatment in, 33–34
    neglect in, 20–22, 33
    normative development in, 106–108
    physical abuse in, 22–23, 33
    psychological abuse in, 26–27
    resources on maltreatment in, 34–35
    sexual abuse in, 26, 31
    theory of mind deficits and maltreatment in, 45
Too Close to Me (Pelzer), 10–11
Toth, S. L., 43, 45
Transitions
    to college, 95–96, 104
    from foster care to independence, 86, 94–95, 100
Trauma
    memory for, 111
    processing of, 53, 114–115
    and resilience, 4
Trauma Affect Regulation: Guide for Education and Therapy (TARGET), 85
Trauma-focused CBT (TF-CBT)
    with adolescents, 85
    with preschoolers, 51, 53
    with school-age children, 68

INDEX

Trauma-Focused CBT for Children and Adolescents (Cohen, Mannarino, & Deblinger), 89
Trauma-sensitive schools, 3, 68–69
Trauma-specific cognitions, 68
Trauma Symptom Inventory—2, 98
Traumatic brain injuries, 23–25
Traumatic stress, dissociation, 49–50
Traumatology, developmental, 4
Treating Traumatic Stress in Children and Adolescents (Blaustein & Kinniburgh), 89
Trickett, P. K., 76
Trust, 57–58, 96, 100
Turner, H., 77
Type 2 diabetes, 6

Understanding
  of abuse, 33
  empathic, 97–98
Unsmiling Faces (Koplow), 53

Very young childhood. *See* Infancy; Toddlerhood
Victimization
  measures of, 104
  poly-, 76
  re-, 81, 83, 87
  sexual, 77–78, 81, 97

Victimology, developmental, 4
Violence, exposure to
  developmental impact of, 112–115
  disruptions to developmental processes from, 109–111
  domestic violence, 41
  and social cognition, 45
  and timing of puberty, 61

Washington state, trauma-sensitive schools in, 68
Women. *See also* Girls
  sexual victimization of, 97
  substance abuse by, 98
  vulnerability of, 104
World Health Organization, 78

Yoerger, K., 65
Young adulthood. *See* Emerging adulthood
Young Children and Trauma (Osofsky), 35

Zabin, L. S., 59, 60
Zeanah, C. H., 35
Zero-tolerance policies, for misbehavior, 70–71
Zero to Three, 35
Zurbriggen, E. L., 96–97

About the Authors

Kathryn Becker-Blease, PhD, is a developmental psychologist and an assistant professor in the School of Psychological Science at Oregon State University. Her major research interests include developmental traumatology—how trauma affects people at different stages of the life course and how prior trauma affects people as they develop over the lifespan. She has published articles on children's trauma as well as on ethical ways to research child abuse and other trauma in journals including *American Psychologist*, *Science*, and *Child Development.* Dr. Becker-Blease has more recently developed a research interest in the science of teaching and learning, including interventions to boost student performance and adaptive learning. She is currently working on a National Science Foundation–funded project to develop and evaluate new educational materials to teach college students research design and graph reading. Her newest work focuses on trauma-informed academic interventions to support academic success for college students who have experienced child abuse, sexual assault, and other trauma.

Patricia K. Kerig, PhD, received her doctorate in clinical psychology from the University of California at Berkeley and currently is a professor and director of clinical training in the Department of Psychology at the University of Utah. She is the author of more than 100 books, chapters, and scientific papers devoted to understanding the factors that predict risk, recovery, and resilience among children and families coping with adversity and traumatic stress, including a textbook, *Developmental Psychopathology*, now in its sixth edition, and a forthcoming book to be published by the American Psychological Association on the role of relationships as sources of risk and resilience for girls on the pathway to delinquency. She is an associate editor of the *Journal of Traumatic Stress* and serves on the editorial boards of several other journals. In addition to her teaching, clinical work, and research devoted to investigating the mechanisms accounting for the link between trauma and youth outcomes, Dr. Kerig is on the faculty of the Center for Trauma Recovery and Juvenile Justice of the National Child Traumatic Stress Network, whose mission is to disseminate trauma-informed assessment and intervention strategies to the juvenile justice system and the youth and families it serves.